CAMBRIDGE LIBRARY COLLECTION

Books of enduring scholarly value

Botany and Horticulture

Until the nineteenth century, the investigation of natural phenomena, plants and animals was considered either the preserve of elite scholars or a pastime for the leisured upper classes. As increasing academic rigour and systematisation was brought to the study of 'natural history', its subdisciplines were adopted into university curricula, and learned societies (such as the Royal Horticultural Society, founded in 1804) were established to support research in these areas. A related development was strong enthusiasm for exotic garden plants, which resulted in plant collecting expeditions to every corner of the globe, sometimes with tragic consequences. This series includes accounts of some of those expeditions, detailed reference works on the flora of different regions, and practical advice for amateur and professional gardeners.

A Garden of Pleasure

Eleanor Vere Boyle (1825–1916), who re-created the gardens of Huntercombe Manor in Berkshire in the 1870s, was a talented artist as well as an author, illustrating both poetry and books for children. From an aristocratic family, and in later life a friend of Queen Alexandra, she produced sketches and watercolours admired by Ruskin and Landseer, and Tennyson and Bulwer Lytton contributed to her anthologies of poetry. One of a number of late nineteenth-century female writers on gardens (many of whose works have been reissued in this series), she was interested in the natural history of the garden rather than in botanical principles. This work, published in 1895, describes the sights, sounds and smells of her garden through the seasons of 1894, with frequent digressions on the weather, birds and animals, the folklore connected with individual plants, literary references, and observations on other gardens visited, in both Britain and Europe.

Cambridge University Press has long been a pioneer in the reissuing of out-of-print titles from its own backlist, producing digital reprints of books that are still sought after by scholars and students but could not be reprinted economically using traditional technology. The Cambridge Library Collection extends this activity to a wider range of books which are still of importance to researchers and professionals, either for the source material they contain, or as landmarks in the history of their academic discipline.

Drawing from the world-renowned collections in the Cambridge University Library and other partner libraries, and guided by the advice of experts in each subject area, Cambridge University Press is using state-of-the-art scanning machines in its own Printing House to capture the content of each book selected for inclusion. The files are processed to give a consistently clear, crisp image, and the books finished to the high quality standard for which the Press is recognised around the world. The latest print-on-demand technology ensures that the books will remain available indefinitely, and that orders for single or multiple copies can quickly be supplied.

The Cambridge Library Collection brings back to life books of enduring scholarly value (including out-of-copyright works originally issued by other publishers) across a wide range of disciplines in the humanities and social sciences and in science and technology.

A Garden of Pleasure

E.V. BOYLE

CAMBRIDGE
UNIVERSITY PRESS

CAMBRIDGE
UNIVERSITY PRESS

University Printing House, Cambridge, CB2 8BS, United Kingdom

Cambridge University Press is part of the University of Cambridge.

It furthers the University's mission by disseminating knowledge in the pursuit of education, learning and research at the highest international levels of excellence.

www.cambridge.org
Information on this title: www.cambridge.org/9781108076609

This edition first published 1895
This digitally printed version 2015

ISBN 978-1-108-07660-9 Paperback

A GARDEN OF PLEASURE

A GARDEN OF PLEASURE

BY

E. V. B.

Author of ' Days and Hours in a Garden,'
' Ros Rosarum,' etc.

' Who loves a garden, still his Eden keeps.'

A. ALCOTT. 1799

LONDON

ELLIOT STOCK, 62 PATERNOSTER ROW, E.C.

1895

DEDICATED

TO MY ELDEST GRANDCHILD, CECIL
ALBINIA ARBUTHNOT, WHOSE DELIGHT
IS IN THE GARDEN, AND WHO MADE
IT THE EDEN OF HER CHILDHOOD.

CONTENTS

PREFACE

Since a preface is said to be a necessary evil, it may perhaps be utilised as a means for the embodying of a few notes on subjects not contained in the book itself. Among these, it should be explained that those flowers—wild or cultivated—whose outlines face first pages of the months, are not supposed to follow in any order of succession as to their proper flowering seasons. They were drawn solely for pure love of them, and were arranged wheresoever they seemed to suit the best.

On finally looking through the proof sheets, the writer has to confess to a disappointing sense of inadequacy ; a pervading, uneasy impression of how poor a thing after all these slight garden records are. The flowers named in them so few—so scanty the attempted portrayal of them! Most emphatically so, when I see the sun-bright garden in all the joy and glory of this royal month of May—now, with Nature at full flood and flow of Spring! with the great elms in the background, half-drest in a fairy garment of budding green. The severity and fatal length of the long winter endured in the garden—though many a tender shrub and plant has died of it—is forgotten in a moment; and indeed it seems on the whole almost to have inspired fresh life and vigour of growth in those delicious things which we call Spring flowers. The rich abundance of our early favourites this year is undiminished. Though long in coming, now that they are here at last they seem more brilliantly beautiful than ever. If any long-loved habitual pleasure of the garden fails to-day, it is that birds are fewer. There are fewer thrushes, and we miss the rapture of their music. Blackbirds must know the secret of some less precarious means of living, for they are as numerous as ever. Yet somehow Merula's magic note is, or so it seems to me, less wholly dear than is the singing of the thrush. The air he sings is so brief, the burden of it so sad! He only sings over

and over, ' *Di Memoria nudrirsi, piu che di speme !* ' ' *I
live on Memory more than hope.*' *Of course he does not
mean it in the least!* but so the tune wears on in
sad, sweet, iteration. In the winter, after Christmas,
the holly trees in the garden shone scarlet, loaded as they
were with berries. We had planned to cut away several
branches of them, but until the birds had stript the fruit,
the gardener's knife was not to be lifted for the pruning.
Yet scarcely had ' *the wise thrush* ' begun to feast, when
down there swooped upon the hollies such flocks of field-
fares from the open country that, in a day the trees
were bare. So the poor throstles—to whom of right
the garden fruits belong—starved and were found dead
in numbers. The motto of wild Nature is always neces-
sarily, ' *Live, and let die who may.*' And thus there
is many a small tragedy enacted often, in the garden.
One of the most pathetic perhaps, when a tiny mother-
bird was found dead in a thorny brier, pierced to the
heart by thorns in the Rose-Home of her choice.*

At this very time, as I write, through the open
window comes fitfully the complaint of a solitary dove

who sits all day alone in the great red horse-chestnut.
His story is a sad one.   On a cold March day, twelve
months ago, a ring-dove appeared no one knows whence
and timidly presented himself outside the garden porch.
The bird was lame and hungry, and very shy; but
after three weeks of persevering attention from us, he
grew fat and tame, and came regularly to feed with
the pigeons. Very soon he found a mate, and brought
her also with him to feed. Then they made a nest
in the red chestnut tree, and in due time the pair
brought a fine young one to be admired and fed at
the door.   Then all three flew away to the woods.
Again, last March, the Dove reappeared one day, and
his mate was with him and the young one too. But
they only stayed a day, and never returned.   And
now the widowed dove sits all day in the chestnut
tree, and calls and calls. From early morning till
late afternoon the plaintive cry is heard: the poor
bird is forsaken, and it is plain that life for him has
lost its interest. Another song comes now and again
from far off among the leaves; and as I listen to

the unutterable sweetness of that sylvan note, the old long-remembered lines recur and keep time with the wood-pigeon's music.

> *' I heard a stock-dove sing or say*
> *His homely tale this very day ;*
> *His voice was buried among trees*
> *Yet to be come at by the breeze :*
> *He did not cease, but cooed, and cooed ;*
> *And somewhat pensively he wooed.*
> *He sang of love with quiet blending,*
> *Slow to begin and never ending,*
> *Of serious faith and inward glee,*
> *That was the song—the song for me.'* *

Heavily has the great frost told on evergreens in the garden. The yew hedges which are our pride, look thin and seared. There is scarce a berberis left alive, and we shall sorely miss those exquisite carpets of yellow and orange which summer by summer did use to spread beneath the shrubs when their little gold bells drop; and there will be no berries ripening in purple bloom. And lavender, on which we set such store, has also suffered, so that the harvest of its fragrant yield will be less rich this year than ever we remember.

*　　　 * Wordsworth.*

*Yet counting all the change and loss that the passing
of the seasons has brought, since those other ' Days and
Hours in a Garden' of more than ten years ago—
enough remains of beauty and delight for us to feel
joyously as ever, the 'ver perpetuum' that irradiates
the garden—whether it be small or great—the Garden
that we call our own.   Of that beloved spot well may
it be said,*

> *' An hour with thee !—when earliest day*
> *Dapples with gold the eastern grey,*
> *Oh, what can frame my mind to bear*
> *The toil and tumult, cark and care,*
> *New griefs, which coming hours unfold,*
> *And sad remembrance of the old ?*
> > *One hour with thee !*
>
> *One hour with thee !—When sun is set,*
> *Oh, what can teach me to forget*
> *The thankless labours of the day,*
> *The hopes and wishes flung away ;*
> *. . . . .*
> > *One hour with thee !' **

*Lovers of their garden should have that feeling for
it strong within them, or their love cannot be true.*

And now, departing not from the custom which holds

* *Sir Walter Scott.*

with letters as with prefaces, and by which the last word is wont to be the most important, a word must be said for the Chief Toiler of the garden, in whose hands lies the responsibility of success or failure. Perhaps there may not be many who would choose a gardener on such lines as these : not many would, so to speak, take the candidate into the garden, and pointing to a cabbage or a currant bush, give the order thus—'Dig a hole and plant that currant head downwards'; and if forthwith the man did as he was told without a word, engage him on the spot! Yet I believe such imperiousness does exist, and then, is fatal to the garden. We may love dearly our flowers; we may know (or think we know), everything about them, and call them all by their names. We may believe we are Master, and that things being done entirely under our own directions everything will grow, and all will be well. Yet nevertheless nothing will grow, nothing will be well unless the gardener is also in a sense, on his side, master. When his worth is ascertained, give him a free hand over all affairs which come specially under his control.

Give him a living interest in the garden by letting him exercise his taste (subject always to yours), in planting and in arrangement of colours, etc., and by showing your own constant interest in it ; and if the man be possessed of good Intelligence and Experience, if his heart is in his work, if he has it in him to Succeed, succeed he will.   The garden and the gardener will grow as it were, to understand one another, and you to trust and understand them both, while your content and gladness in the garden will increase and grow with the year's increase.

And here a grateful tribute must find place, for the Gardener, JESSE FOULK, by whose rare skill this plot grew into a Garden of Pleasure, whose ceaseless care has maintained its charm for three-and-twenty summers, and who completes the Thirtieth year of his devoted service on the 22nd of May : with which well-omened date I close my Preface.

ELEANOR VERE BOYLE.

HUNTERCOMBE MANOR,
  May, 1895.

JANUARY

A

I

JANUARY

' Life is a road, at either end a gate,
  The gate of Life behind—of Death beyond.
Love guards the path and guides us all the way,
  As through a garden where calm Hope doth rest.'
                                    G. F. Bodley.

JANUARY 1894.—At last the white snow
sheet is lifted, and we draw a breath
of relief as it were, after the tension of a
long long winter. It was not really long,
however, it only lasted about three weeks
or so. And there have been brilliant sun-
shines, and early morning splendours were
not rare, when the lawns became wide
diamond-fields, as pure and sparkling as
winter's frost could freeze them. Splendours also there have been, of sunset skies
whose glory died not until the utmost
remotest glow of green had faded into
grey. Wondrous joys such as these are,

must be now foregone; for they perforce
have waned with the frosty nights, and
scarcely a regret goes with them, so happy
is the feeling of the warmer air, and the
smell of the grass set free at last from the
ice-king's iron grip. Instantly, upon his
departure, little sharp blades of crocus,
with the broader pale green shafts of
daffodil have arisen inches above ground,
and ' daisies, pearled Arcturi of the earth,'
will soon be born among the grass. Even
in the gentian border there appears one
poor bell of pinched and sickly blue,
gleaming faintly among its frost-tainted
leaves.

The first anxious visit after such severity
of frost, is of course paid to the little
clump of Olearia, near the western end of
the rockery. A dozen or so of plants
were grown from tiny cuttings, sent from
the Isle of Wight, two years and a half ago.
After most tender nursing they grew into
fine young plants, as large as an ordinary
lavender bush of the same age, and were
duly planted out. Last summer they were
literally white all over with little daisy

flowers. In the autumn (at the time that they were sheltered carefully under thick green spruce branches), each little spray and twig was loaded with a mass of buds just formed.

Alas ! a glance underneath the covering at once betrayed the irremediable hurts our pets had suffered. They were all brown and grey, diffusing a sort of sickly fragrance, not perceptible in their summers of full strength and inflorescence. It has to be confessed, that our garden lies too low, and is not sufficiently dry, to suit some things.

Gentians seem to be always blowing : the vitality of them is marvellous; there was one on a patch niched snugly in the rock garden, that bloomed on for ever! It displayed its ultramarine magnificence every day for fully six weeks. Every day when the sun shone, I did homage to it. Sometimes the blue of it was so velvety, so brilliant, that one could scarce forbear to stoop and kiss its open face ! I find this in my garden diary: 'Oct. 15. A large blue gentian on Roman walk. It shuts up when very cold, and opens wide in the sun at noon.' 'Nov. 18. The Gentian there still.' On Nov. 27, 'Poor little gentian has begun to fade;' and then, Dec. 1, 'The Gentian is withered away.' It grew on a glossy-leaved, vigorous root, sheltered by a flat stone ledge, in a pocket half way up the bank, facing due south. This strange flower, with its movements of opening and closing, and its colour-changes of expression, resembled almost some live sea-creature. In May the plant is sure to bloom again, between great cushions of pink and snowy phlox Nelsonii. But then, its natural life will not last for more than a week or two.

It is like a 'far-off melody,' to return in thought from the grand deep azure gentian of the mountain-side or the garden, to its little sister of our own wild English heaths. It was near the sea coast where first we met, on one of the loveliest of miniature moors, where a sudden hollow hides the unsightly crowd of surrounding villas. The September sun shone down in softened brilliance, and the blowing breeze put one

in mind of Scotland. The brown heath-
land glowed with autumn-flowering furze;
that low creeping kind which inter-threads
among the heather, and glows in the sunshine like embroidery of the richest gold.
There remained still some scattered tufts
of pink bell-heather and ling; green-grey
lichen at their roots, variegated with
delicious tones the all-prevailing brown.

Suddenly, low among the moss, in a wet
boggy spot, between two heathery fir-
crowned braes, I became aware of a soft
gleam of blue. It was the pale azure of
wild gentian. The flowers were opened
wide in all their gentle loveliness, drinking
in the full joy of mid-day.

It may not be rare, I believe it to be only
what is called 'local,' but to me it was
absolutely new. It is very delicate and
shy—and how exquisite is its dream-like
reflex of that other deep blue dweller on
the Alps! The place where it grew was
still, as might be any moorland solitude
miles away from everybody. Only an in-
distinct low murmur either of the sea or
noises of the town, mingled with light

whisperings among the pine tops, floated through the air around. Above the olive-green and tawny sedges where these earth stars shone, each one single and alone on its short upright stalk, there came an Atalanta butterfly leisurely wandering across the valley. . . . I hope it was not a very brutal impulse that moved me to nip off and gather into a little bunch every one of those wild Gentian flowers, and take them carefully away! Some covetous eye was almost sure to spy them out, some heedless hand would pull up the roots and carry them away to perish. But it seemed rather like doing evil that good might come!

More than nine years have slipped by since the last of these garden notes in September 1883. A new series was begun in the February following, breaking off before November. Three months are now worked in to complete the twelve. Through all these days and hours, changes of every kind have passed over the old Buckinghamshire garden. Nine times has Spring bloomed and ripened into summer there.

Summer suns have burned and failed;
Autumn leaves have fallen in showers of
rustling gold, and winter·winds have swept
them away. Old trees are gone and new
trees have been planted, and everywhere
about the place reigns the inevitable law of
change. Old paths have been turned,
flower-beds here and there have been
turfed over, or new ones made. Yet now
things seem as if they ought always to
have been just so, and no other way at
all ! A new sundial, put together with
old carved stones and cement, now stands
upon the east lawn between the Sequoia
gigantea, and the Cedar. Already it wears
the look of having stood there for years.
There is a motto worked upon the steps
in Latin : it means, ' Light and shade in
turn, but Love always.' Round the top,
just below the dial, three lions walk with
solemn step from the sun-rising southward,
towards the east again.

The chiefest change of all, is the creation
of Peach Corner. On the sunny side of a
very old brick wall which had probably
formed the boundary between the garden

and the stable yard in former days, lay a rubbishy square plot of ground. Here were summered out the Camellias and Azaleas etc., etc. Here also was the place of dilapidated frames, and all sorts of orra* plants, and empty flower-pots. Old Peach trees were trained on the wall, and we used to think that peaches reddened riper there than on other walls. But the Peach trees kept on decaying year by year, making less hard the decision to remove them. When the time came for destroying the bit of old brick work—that was a harder matter ; not undertaken until after endless hesitations, yet not regretted since. The walk on the north side used to end in gloomy shade under a very large old Phylleria, growing in a narrow border full of melancholy ferns. Now, a much-needed thoroughfare is gained by carrying on the walk beyond. The great Phylleria breathes freer now, rejoicing in the sun which, for the first time warms its rugged old grey stem. Excepting upon its umbrageous

* 'Orra,' a Scotch word used for anything laid anywhere out of the way.

upper half, above the wall, this tree had never seen the sun since George Evelyn planted the row of Phyllereas, in imitation apparently of that at his cousin's place at Wotton.

Smooth bare poles alone remain of all the others : yet such is their vitality, although to all appearance they have long been dead, that from the roots have sprung a thicket of young wood, so luxuriant as almost to hide the barren decay of the parent stems. Since Peach Corner commended itself as a pleasant name for the new 'improvement,' after the place was cleared fresh soil filled in and the walk extended—to justify the title three double blossomed standard peach trees, are placed there in the grass. In the remnant of old wall, arched openings have been worked with a lattice of thin wire strained across, up which Mina lobata climbed joyously last summer to the very top, and then fell over, breaking in a rich mantling of leaf, light and lovely as folds of green lace might be. When mina lobata starts to grow, about the middle or

end of August, nobody else can possibly
climb so fast.   Her flower is of no account ;
but it no more is needed than the leaves
to which belong so much of grace and
charm.   In a sunny angle of Peach
Corner, there is a William Richardson
rose.   Beautiful as it is, it comes not
near, nor never will, to the wonder of
one that grew in the gardens of La
Mortola, nearly twenty feet high, and
crowned with hundreds of orange-hearted
roses.   The rose called, 'Idèale,' delights
and disappoints by turns in the opposite
corner.   In the border near them, flourished
in the later days of summer, a strange
black dahlia.

It is altogether unlike its name, and yet
dahlia it is most certainly, by the leaves
and the stiff long stalk, by the bud and the
flower and the root.   At first sight, you
would say it was a potentilla of unusual
size.   For a *dahlia*, it is very small indeed ;
and the velvet-black of it never fails to
charm, whether growing in the open border
or mixed in when cut, with very bright
late-blooming flowers.   In late summer

days, Peach Corner is crowded with delicious things; there is yellow Cassia,
luxuriantly gay throughout the day, and
after sunset so forlorn with drooping leaves
shut close together like the sensitive plant.

Nicotiana, whose dejection lasts all the
while that Cassia has her day, but who
breaks forth in white shining stars at dusk,
cobalt Comelina and sweet verbena and
apple-scented salvia dotted over with a
tiny scarlet flower, and pale blue daisies.
There is an edging of Sea-Pink or Thrift.
(Why is it Thrift? Is it because it thrives
everywhere, in the richest or the poorest
soil?) In another part of the garden there
is a strip of a variety that glows with a
deeper tone of pink. These came from a
garden in the Highlands, where the sunny
middle walk, edged with Sea-Pink, led up
to an arbour, overgrown with convolvulus
and white honeysuckle, and surrounded by
sweet peas. No one ever sits in an arbour
now-a-days. I think they are never made
now, and dear old Mrs Sherwood's story in
that delicious fifty years' ago penny series
of hers (tiny little books in various coloured

paper covers), entitled 'The Lady in the Arbour,' could not have been written now. In the woodcut frontispiece, the lady, drest in a scanty short-waisted gown, a cap on her head, and a narrow shawl pinned round her shoulders, sits in the arbour with a book on her knee. It is a prim, precise looking latticed arbour, with no wild garlanding of anything about it. Behind is a bit of old broken park paling, and a very black wood. Through a gap in the paling creeps a little child, as if intent on making its way to the lady in the arbour. I think the idea was, that the lady waited there every morning for the wood-cutter's child to read to it from the Bible on her lap. Not much, perhaps, in the simple little story to interest a child-reader. The charm must have lain in that picture of the gap, with its infinite suggestions of all that might lie beyond the wood, and of all there might be on the other side, of moss or snail-shells, or velvety field mouse among the withered leaves and sticks.

What would I not give to see again

those little penny books with their Bewick-
like woodcuts ! Alas ! I seek them in vain.
I can recall a few titles such as 'The
Rosebuds,' 'The Little Dog Flora, and
her Silver Bell,' 'The Two Dolls,' 'The
Snow,' 'Sophronia and her Kitten.' Very
little hope remains of copies of these or any
others ever rewarding my long search. But
we have wandered far from Peach Corner.
Through the glass walls of the green-house
which bounds one side, come gleams of
scarlet geranium and of red winter carnations. The raised border alongside is
this year filled with double violets. They
are the dark purple kind that are never
met with now. Their scent is powerful;
and if a drawback to their cultivation
exists, it is only that their stalks are too
short. Aubretia hangs over the stone
edges of this violet bed, and we half-per-
ceive behind the glass, a grove of arum
lillies, with all the promise of their long
spirals soon to untwist and open out in
broad patches of ivory white.

The great Rhynchospermum jasminoides,
which for years had filled up one corner

of the house is dead.   Early summer
used to clothe it in white waxen clusters,
for our delight.   Both the old and the
new aubretias are here ; the new grows
the strongest, but the colour of it is too
much mixt with red to please so greatly
as the old.   When the common aubretia
begins to show in lilac upon its compact
mass of grey-green cushion, the image
of a never-forgotten April evening at
Farringford fails not to return to me,
with all the freshness of a dearly cherished
memory.

The straight garden path sloped gently
upwards to an open summer-house, where
sat the Poet Laureate, discoursing with his
friends.

It was the season when aubretia shone
in all the bloom of her lilac loveliness, up
and down the borders.   Later on, white
lilies would rise in tall groups at the back.
In the trees all around, thrushes and
blackbirds were celebrating the early spring
at the top of their voices.   The hour was
late, and efforts were ineffectually made
to persuade him to return to the house.

But the air was so balmy, and he was so
happy sitting there, in the garden, enjoying
the soft glow of evening light,—that go
into the house he would not. Presently
however, as he saw the sky grow grey and
misty, wiser counsels prevailed, and then
he rose and left the garden. As we slowly
wended to the house along the deeply
shadowed path between the trees, he
pointed to some bushes of the small leaved
laurel growing amongst the others. They
were his favourites he said : the Victor's
Laurel of ancient Greece, and he told of
how they loved the shade, and grew the
best underneath thick trees.

Well is it for us that no voice whispers to
the heart, sometimes when we say farewell,
' It is the last time, nevermore.' It was the
last time I ever saw the beloved poet; a
few months passed by, and then the world
was poorer by the loss of him who had
been given to live so long his noble poet's
life amongst us, ' unhasting, unresting like
a star ; ' a star that shines forever now, in
' heaven's clear calm.'

Outside the greenhouse door, a small

B

patch of Guernsey lilies grow and thrive.
When I am absent at the time of their flowering, a box containing one or two blooms,
most beautifully pink, is sure to reach me
wherever I may be. In the small Propa-
gating House near by, Dendrobium nobilis
is richly flowering. I believe this dendrobium to be the oldest variety known in
England, and our plant has flourished with
us for well nigh forty years, having accom-
panied us from the old Somerset home.
Beside it in delicious contrast, are many
clusters of amber-fringed D. fimbriata.
The vitality of Nobilis is so strong, that
the flower will survive without water, or
even worn as a ' button-hole ' for almost
the whole length of a day. There is an
interesting young tree in a small pot in
this house, an infant Dragon Tree. It is
a seedling from Tenerife, where, till lately,
lived that ancient Dragon, recorded to
have seen at least two thousand years.
They tell me that in about a century, our
specimen may have attained the height of
four feet. Where shall all we be then?
The most interesting inhabitant of this

'Touch us gently, Time !
We've not proud nor soaring wings
Our ambition, *our* content
Lies in simple things,
Humble voyagers are We,
O'er life's dim unsounded sea,
Seeking only some calm clime :—
Touch us gently, Time !'

Barry Cornwall.

house, however, is a large Eft. I found
him one day outside the door, in a puddle
of rain, asking, as plain as words, to be al-
lowed to get inside to be warm.   So I took
the clammy creature up, and placed him
within amongst the ferns and pebbles, and
never since has he vouchsafed us a single
glimpse of himself. This is a draw-back,
for he is extremely handsome.   Black,
with orange spots, and orange throat.
Efts of this kind are not uncommon,
though, perhaps, seldom seen so large as
our friend, who measured something like
ten inches.   They are found under stones
in dampish places, mostly in churchyards.
The small dry brown efts, that sometimes walk in at the door from the garden,
are not so handsome, but certainly are
pleasanter to handle, and the expression
of their face is rather pathetic.

Once, and once only, in the far past,
I found a Golden Eft ! It must have been
the Queen eft, and it dwelt in one of
the most fascinating ponds on Wimbledon
Common. The colour was purest yellow-
gold, and near its head it wore beautiful

crested gills. There exists a curious and almost universal ignorance about these our lowly fellow - creatures ; about all ‘ reptiles ’ indeed.

A boy who had ‘ finished his education ’ at school, invited us the other day to come and look at a leech. The ‘ leech ’ turned out to be an eft (or as the country people say, an ‘ effet ’). Long ago, snakes abounded in the garden at certain seasons of the year. They were most harmless snakes, but never are they seen now, so determined has been the enmity against them, so constantly have they been destroyed whenever silly enough to let themselves be seen. Once, I met a beauty four feet long, gliding through the half open orchard gate, into the stable yard. And in those days, I dreamed a dream one night of a great snake-fight raging in the path near the hedge in the House meadow. Next morning the dream was verified, for walking along that path, on the very spot where the visionary fight took place, I came upon the broken up bodies and bones of three snakes. They

must have been destroyed by some one
with a stick who had caught them un-
awares while in the blind fury of deadly
combat.   I think these beautiful creatures
are scarcer everywhere than in former
days.   It is very long since I have rejoiced
at the sight of a snake in some wild place,
slipping through the long green grass—'a
beauteous wreath with melancholy eyes '—
or undulating across a streamlet.

Harmless and graceful however as is
the common snake, an adder is quite a
different affair!   No living creature bears
a more sinister expression.   The form of
the small cruel head, and the faultlessly
regular and even chain-pattern along the
back.   The very shade of cold pale brown
that colours it, and the glassy green of its
under side, seem to bear a wicked look.
One may well fear ' a snake in the grass '
of *that* species!   In the garden, animated
Nature is always as full of charm, (at least
to me!) as are the flowers.   A pair of
small call-ducks wander here at will.   Sir
Francis, the drake, is very handsome :
plumaged like a mallard.   His partner takes

not the slightest notice of him. She quite
ignores his devotion, though he follows her
about continually, and scarcely eats himself,
till she has had her fill. One peculiarity
is, that they are essentially dry ducks.
They have a holy horror of water—the
pond in the field which one would suppose
might be such a comfort in hot weather,
they carefully avoid. When it rains, they
waddle inside the porch. And when the
walks and grass happen to be wet, they are
quite uncomfortable, and scramble up on
to any dry place they can find, to be out of
the damp. On the other hand, these ducks
will make believe to wash on the very
dryest gravel, and will clap their wings
and dip as if the gravel were deep waters !
Some very secret inhabitants of the garden
are the hedgehogs; they are scarcely ever
seen but on one day in the year. On
warm June evenings, I begin to watch for
the old mother hedgehog, who never fails
to bring out her young family (almost invariably three) for their first survey of the
wide wide world of green turf, under the
elms, at the northern end of the garden.

The chosen spot is very solitary and far removed, and rarely does the old one permit us to catch the least glimpse of her prickles ! But the three little ones are not so wary. It is very nice to take one of them in one's hand, and peer into the little black face and deep-set sparkling eyes, and feel the soft under-fur and the little cool feet ! One evening however, (there were but two that summer) the young ones rolled up instantly upon hearing footsteps : and although a watch was kept at a distance for full twenty minutes, the little prickleys never moved. So we left them to themselves.

All winter through, up to the end of March, or longer, cocoa-nuts hang from the Rose Arches for the titmice. The hole is always made in the lower part, so as to discourage the sparrows, who do not fancy hanging head downwards. (It is not that they couldn't do it, for there is nothing they cannot do if they try !) For a long time they did not understand that cocoa-nut was good. But unfortunately a nut-hatch let fall some crumbs of it one day :

and then the sparrows found out how nice
it was. At regular intervals in the short
winter days, the titmice come to feed—
about four of each kind. There is the
great tomtit, masterful and quarrelsome.
The cole-tit, very brisk and persevering;
the little blue-cap, most lovely and timid
and yielding in its ways, and that other tit
which is almost the cole-tit with a differ-
ence. It may be the male cole, or it may
be the Nun. It was on a morning in last
June that a mother cole-tit—tiny and
fascinating little mite !—brought out her
newly flown brood to introduce them
to me and the cocoa-nuts. I watched
from the oak-room window, which exactly
faces the line of rose arches. The little
mother pecked out little beakfuls of nut,
darting to and fro with flits and flirts of
wings and tail, feeding the young, and
trying to teach them how to get at the
food for themselves. After a time they
all flew ; and for several minutes the side
of the yew hedge was alive with minute
tits climbing and clinging all over it.
Then they got back to the nuts, and one

tiny creature in a futile way tried to imitate
its parent.   But hanging topsy-turvy is
rather an impossible trick for a beginner,
so it didn't try any more, but set to
work at the green-fly on the rose-shoots.
The young tit family did not appear
again, but a nut-hatch brought her one
chick for several mornings to the rose
arches.

It was nearly as big as its mother, and
seemed all head and shoulders.   It sat
shivering and fluttering, while she dug at
the nut, every few moments extracting a
morsel, and stuffing it down the chick's
throat.   It did not attempt to dig for
itself ; when it flew off, one saw how
strong on the wing it was.   When the nut
is fresh, shreds fly about as the nut-hatch
hacks it, and then the birds become quite
playful ; dashing after the flying fragments
and catching them in the air before they
fall.

FEBRUARY

II

FEBRUARY, 1884

'Gloomy winter's now awa'.'

SUDDENLY, without any warning as it were, winter is away. There's a new sound in the air, 'a new face at the door.' This is Sunday and the sound is the rooks' consultation in the tops of the great Elms (they always arrange matters on a Sunday), while in the garden, the air seems full of the voices of birds. Through the budding branches and the thickness of the winter greens is woven a network of melody, where a thousand little finches twitter, and blackbirds and thrushes just lightly touch their long silent notes. And there's a vision of the sweetest face in all the world—the first pale glimpse of Spring with her snowdrop crown. It was but yesterday the Snowdrops had

scarce begun to show in silvery points above
the earth—to-day the slender stalks have
risen two inches high! There are pure
white double primroses and a few coloured,
in every part of the garden, where so late
as yesterday there seemed to be none.
Even the yellow of a winter aconite, or
the blue of scyllas, begin to show here
and there. I do not know if the sap does
actually rise at the touch of spring, but
there has come a fresher green in the
broad blue-green iris leaves, and the ends
of the long rose sprays are flushed with
emerald, and a warmer green glows through
the prickly junipers. This first awaken-
ing comes rather later than usual. Though
the season has been so mild, it was unusually dark, and in my garden diary for
December I find fifteen days marked ' very
dark.' In January there were indeed days
when we beheld the sun, but it has been
mostly a reign of darkness, and earth's
stars, which are the flowers, are few.

These Snowdrops! year after year they
come again to test our appreciation of form
and simplicity, and every year their

triumph is assured. I challenge you to
show me the grandest bell-flower born of
tropic suns that can compare in its attri-
butes of perfect grace with our English
snowdrop. I mean the large old single
snowdrop—I will have nothing to do with
the double, as a snowdrop. The snowdrop
is in itself a lesson of form and colour—
from the straight, long oval of the tube, out
of which spring three sweet oval lobes, to
the delicate pencilling in Nature's loveliest
green of the threefold inner cup. And you
will observe there is no over-luxuriant
fulness, all is severely, tenderly restrained,
as are the lines of a Greek statue. And
then the colour! it is pure as fresh-fallen
snow upon an alpine peak. The hanging
of the bell, too, is a wonder of firm lightness,
so light that with a breath it swings, so
strong it will upbear the snow-drift. One
lovely detail must not be forgotten : this
is the folding inwards of the lobes along
each outer edge, giving a peculiar grace
which hard lines here could never have.
But an attempt to describe the snowdrop
must fail; I know of no words simple

enough, nor any language rich enough to give its perfect beauty. Dear innocent flower of home! There are exiles under skies of eastern drouth whose brave hearts faint with longing if they do but for a moment dwell upon the thought of your cold loveliness.

FEBRUARY 14.—The happy birds are keeping St Valentine's Day, and I have found an Echo! There seems ever a weird charm in the mysterious presence which makes such arbitrary choice of some special spot, building or rock, and lives there for ever silent and unknown until awoke by chance, and then is so warily on the watch, ever ready to start up and mock the passer-by with a hollow imitation of his voice or footstep. Doubtless there is some scientific explanation, but it does really seem that Echo is a capricious being, and will come and go much as she pleases; else why is it that, after haunting a place for years, she will sometimes disappear one day without rhyme or reason, and never come back? I have not thought of it for

"Pride of the dewy glade"

C

many a year; but at this moment I remember like yesterday a lovely echo, or
group of echoes, somewhere in Switzerland, I think it was on the Grindelwald,
within view of the Great Scheideck. A
man played a little tune on an immense
shepherd's horn. The travellers listened
and after a pause Echo gave back the air
note for note with clear and sweet preci-
sion; and then from hill to hill her hermit
sisters took up the music over and over
again till the sounds became small and far,
dying away in a fairy-like *diminuendo*.
That is how memory recalls to me the
beautiful Fairy of the Scheideck Pass. But
our new-comer dwells somewhere near the
end of a brick wall partly covered with
ivy. She, too, is a fairy, but of coarser
mould, and she can only repeat once. I
was startled by the sudden mockery early
one morning as I called my dog, and I can
solemnly affirm that this Echo has only
just arrived and settled in the wall; for
close by, it is an almost daily occurrence to
turn and call the dog in, before shutting
the garden gate and we have never before

heard her voice. Echoes are rare here on
the flat. We had one in a gable of the
house, but she went away or was lost when
the yew hedges were planted. In some
counties they say the bulls in the fields are
made savage by hearing their own cries
re - echoing from the woods and hills
around.

We have had busy days of late trimming
the creepers all round the house. Long
prunings of honeysuckles and jasmine
with leafy splendours of Magnolia, lay in
lavish waste upon the gravel, and the air
was full of the curious pungency of ivy
leaves. Pruning days are my delight,
when the laurel and box are trimmed,
and the aroma of them scents the whole
place, and clipped sprigs fall, and are
spread about, strewing the ground as if for
some garden triumph. One day last spring
(it was on May 12) I thought to try a little
pruning on my own account, and severed
a long healthy branch of vine, which,
when in leaf, would smother a young pomegranate growing on the south wall. I
shall never forget what followed the rash

act. The vine began to bleed ; pure crystal sap welled up, and drop after drop fell fast ; it flowed and flowed and poured from the wound, and never ceased till seven days and nights were past. In the first dismay at seeing this wine of life pour forth I tried to staunch it by binding a handkerchief tightly round. But that availed nothing ; the cambric was drenched in a moment, while down the stem the stream ran on as the poor Vine wasted her blood upon the earth. I felt it was murder, and the vine seemed to me like some hapless human creature bleeding to death ! Through the day I returned again and again, and guiltily crept to the place at night when the moon was shining— and still the wound bled, and the stem of the vine grew black with moisture, and the wood strawberry leaves underneath were full of big drops. At last one happy morning the tree was dry. I believe it is only in spring that a vine will behave like this—and no harm was done ! But for me henceforth, the vine may go unpruned for evermore. The amateur knife does, however, still work usefully on young limes and such-like, keeping the stems smooth and free from buddings out of leaves and twigs, and the Gardener is lenient with my amusements in this line.

In the Wilderness (so we name a rather wild unkept grassy place outside the gates of old Italian ironwork that enclose a broad opening between yew hedges) we have planted climbing roses, and Clematis Jackmanni and Montana at the foot of some useless apple and plum trees. Many old roses are at their best only when thus grown wild, as it were, without the least restraint. Only in this way do they attain their fulness of grace and beauty. And by this kind of growth only can one imagine the sleeping Titania, quite over-canopied with musk roses. A white Noisette left to itself to grow up the stem of our stone pine has grown so immensely in the few years since it was planted as to take complete possession of the tree ; climbing in the richest luxuriance up to the top, and thence hanging down in long rosy wreaths of exquisite lightness. Yet, although in

its season of flowering none would deny
this rose's loveliness, we have hardened our
hearts, and have been cutting away the
half of it, so as entirely to free the foliage
of the pine.   There is many a handsomer
tree we could easier spare from the garden
than the remains of that old Stone Pine.
The interests belonging to it are endless.
There are the great green cones that reign
secure in the widespread umbrella top, and
the brown ones that come down with a
thump on the grass when the wind blows
a gale, and that are good to fill the empty
grates in summer, and to smell of Italy in
winter; and the titmice and wrens and
robins and all manner of small birds that
lodge in its branches, whose ways are so
pleasant and past finding out; and the
curiosity that is never satisfied as to the
enormous white fleshy grubs we sometimes
see them dig out of holes and crannies in
the bark, and carry off in their beaks.
And the long double pine needles which
drop and lie flat all day where they fell,
and bristle upright in the turf next morning after the worms have been pulling

them under all night. All these and countless small matters besides make up a little world of interest in our great Pine. The seeds are collected yearly, and they always grow when sown, and thrive up to a certain age; yet we have not been able to rear any young trees.

In the Boccage there are now two living proofs of the mild weather we have had. The unconscious obstinacy of one of them sometimes makes me smile : it is a Tritoma. December came too soon, and caught the central flower-stalk with its usual pyramid of buds still incomplete. The plant remained in the same position quite unconcerned, and has managed ever since to keep life in the buds, holding itself doggedly upright, and in perfect health, with a sheaf of fresh green leaves about it, and actually surrounding itself with a family of shorter flower-stalks ; and after sometimes looking pale in snow-time or frost, the whole group takes heart again vigorously. With a little sunshine we should see it in nearly as fine bloom as in September. Near the grass walk, glowing in bright pink against the

grey of a shadowy elm-tree background,
there has been for three weeks or more a
large round half-opened Rose : it blooms
at the end of a long summer rose-shoot.
In the wintry winds it has swung to and
fro undismayed. Once or twice I have
seen it crested with frost. The white
crystals fell away and left it bright as ever
when warmer days brought to it a new
warmth of colour. Now it begins to flag;
the pink petals have gradually hardened,
and some of the green leaves are withered;
but yet the half-opened rose endures
bravely, and sometimes shines like a rosy
star. The violet leaves, in sheltered places
under the walls, are just beginning to be
strewn with amethysts; and the double
lilac Marie Louise violets, which we turned
out in the borders, have borne flowers as
large and fragrant as those in the frames
all through the winter. If the old garden-
ing books may be believed, it is quite easy
to double the single purple wild Violet.

MARCH

III

MARCH

'March comes in with an Adder's head,
And goes out with a Peacock's tail.'
Old Saying.

MARCH 12.—I waste my time just now in
observing from the window, a pair of little
blue titmice. They mean to build in the
ivy and roses that cluster round the old
stone pine ; not, I think, in the rustic
bark mansion placed ready for them in a
yew tree hard by. These titmice are the
gracefulest little things imaginable : flitt-
ing about like airy living leaves, their colour
a lovely grey-green flashed with blue. One
never tires of following with the eye their
pretty graceful movements, while they
are hunting in and out of the branches.
Nothing can exceed their animation and
grace as they turn and twist upon a small

square of bacon-fat* made fast to the end of a long string. This dainty, replaced constantly as it wastes, hangs all the winter from the tree for the tomtits' special benefit. They are tame also, and, like all very little birds, are seemingly not able to take in the idea of a large human being. Quite unlike this small fearlessness of titmice is the impudent effrontery of our little ne'er-do-weels—the sparrows. Their familiarity seems to have no touch of kindliness in it. I do not blame them. It is the shape of their blunt coarse beaks, that affects their whole nature! The sparrows' perverseness increases, and the friendlier we are to them, the worse they behave. They tear up into shreds our beautiful purple and yellow crocuses, but mainly the yellow. The white and the lilac are left comparatively unmolested, and they seem to attack the beds only in full sunshine. Crocuses, I feel sure, never before suffered from sparrows as they do this season.

* At the time this was written, in 1884, we had not invented cocoa-nuts—a pleasanter feast, and equally acceptable to the tits.

The Sea Purslane also, which luxuriates
in our warm soil, has been persecuted all
the winter, and is now stripped nearly bare
of leaves. I believe this ferocity (for it is
nothing less) of our sparrows is to be
attributed to the unusual dryness of the
weather following the long drought of
last summer. Want of food it cannot be,
for all our beloved birds have been fed
throughout the winter. Moisture is sought
by them in the honey-drop within the
crocus flower, and in the rather fleshy
foliage of the sea purslane. In the spring
the sparrows will amply pay for the sorrows
they cause us now, and the more sparrows'
nests, the fewer grubs there will be to plague
us. It is remarkable that the Gardener is
not unfriendly to our sparrows. In his
judgment their extreme cleverness hides a
multitude of sins. They have now actually
set to work to master the Indian corn
which we give to the pigeons in the hope
that sparrows will never find the way to
swallow it. Their perseverance in trying to
get at the core of it, without holding down
the grain as anyone else would, with one

foot, is worthy of a better cause. The
sparrow's eye for colour (one would guess
that flaunting yellow would be their chosen
colour!) is not the same as the hive-bee's.
Bees seem to avoid the yellow Crocus,
while they love the white, the purple, and
the striped. I have watched them of late
when the sun has been warm and bright.
I do not know if hive-bees carry on into
the summer their objection to yellow; it is
certain, however, that in sunflower time
the yellow sunflowers are visited by
Humble-bees only. One division of our
crocus enemies has been partly check-
mated by the simple plan of putting in the
bulbs very deep; the mice do not quite so
easily get at them.* Numbers have also
been successfully trapped. Hares, on the
other hand, have annoyed us more than
usual. A long row of fine young wallflowers have been devoured by them,
besides scores of carnations in the Boccage
—the hares and I agreeing in our love for
wallflowers, only *their* fancy is for the

* A more successful plan is to stretch black thread
from little sticks across the flowers.

leaves, not the flowers. Poor hares! It is little consolation for our loss to remember that they were all shot and roasted for dinner, after they had done the mischief!

Charming as masses and lines of crocus are in the borders and parterres, to enjoy them thoroughly they must be growing in the green grass, and they must be spreading themselves wide open to the sunshine at mid-day. The orchard is gay with broad patches of yellow crocus—remnants torn from the field of the Cloth of Gold; and the banks of our tiny watercourse is a long green cloth laid out with services of amethyst and silver cups. Within the garden pure white and golden crocus sprinkle the turf round trees and elsewhere, where their leaves need not be mown off too soon.

All this should be in the past tense, for the crocus has already seen its prime, and the remaining few look pinched under the east wind's bane. How strangely vivid, with how great tenacity, will some very little unimportant scene or feeling sometimes cling to the memory through all the

years! Thus, with February's first purple
crocus, for me unfailingly arises in a far-off
tender light the vision of some forgotten
garden wilderness enclosed with trees,
beyond the town, where my mother and I
once walked together. There, as we rested
under the trees, appeared before us a
solitary purple Crocus, shining on the
grassy lawn! After years, whose number
one scarcely cares to count, that moment's
joy is in sober truth recalled as the most
exquisite of a whole long lifetime.

On the old brick south wall of the
kitchen garden our only plant of Pyrus
japonica is arrayed in finer bloom than
usual. Hardly an inch of brown wood
shows between the clustering red of a
thousand rich and brilliant blossoms. Last
autumn the fruit ripened (or, to be truer,
hardened) upon it in large green apples
of a pippin shape. What an old-fashioned
shrub it is! and how seldom seen but in
old gardens : and how, in these days, one
never thinks of planting a new one. About
the roots of the Pyrus japonica, and along
the narrow border at the foot of the wall,

is a delicious tangle of iris, violets, and rosemary, narcissus of the less common kinds, with many a sweet South-loving plant that has got there one knows not when nor how. Amongst them is a star of Bethlehem, and in the wall itself grow bunches of yellow fumitory (Corydalis lutea) just coming into flower; and there is a seedling holly, and a little starved yew niched in a cranny near the top, and there are patterns in grey lichen scrawled upon the red brick. The polyanthus narcissus, under the wall—roots that have been turned out of the greenhouse after flowering in days gone by—are luxuriantly beautiful this season. Their petals are the clearest yellow, and the cups deep orange, most richly scented. The orange centres seem to gather in and hoard all the sunshine that has ever shone upon them, giving it out again in living sun-gold, even in dullest weather.

The delicate lilac flowers of Iris ensata, sheltered among the thick-growing bushes of dark green leaves, are blooming abundantly. There have been hundreds of

D

blossoms, and we have never been without them since December, for we had them under glass all January till February, when we began to perceive a lilac glow among the leaves in the open air. These Irises bloom here at precisely the same time with those of the same kind in their own warm sun-steeped land. They could not flower here so early but for the sheafs of sheltering leaves which almost hide them from sight. Few things look more charming for the table than the transiently perfumed iris ensata! One evening we had them arranged in knots, with mignonette and sprays of lemon-scented pelargonium, toned with the brown of Cryptomeria elegans. One often hears a gardener's arrangement of flowers reviled as stiff, or garish; yet this lovely contrast of lilac, green, and brown was only a gardener's nosegay! As a decoration it might have been deemed pallid, but for the presence of glasses filled with deep coloured primroses, Dog-tooth violets, and Glory of the snow, all resting against the brown. The tips of Cryptomeria used in this way are neither stiff nor heavy, but full of the lightest grace.

MARCH 21.—Spring began this morning *
before 6 A.M. The tame robin sang such
a brilliant brief fantasia in the magnolia just
outside my window, that when the shutters
were opened it was a surprise to see heavy
snow falling. Snow is as good as change
of scene to us home-keeping folk. Our
view from the windows is transformed.
The large Ilex oak drooping under its
load of snow looks more like a yew, or
some kind of fir tree. The outline and
character of the Stone pine is entirely
changed. 'Deborah' and the sun dial
stand out boldly sculptured in black and
white, as every day they certainly are not.
The parterre with its crocuses is gone;
the grass and the walks are nowhere.
Branching elms in the background are
almost as much increased in size by the
snow crystalising over every slender twig,
as in summer by their leafy millions. But
all this proved only a dissolving view : by
noon the grass appeared again, green as

* Spring is said to commence 21st March.

an emerald, and the thrushes were loudly
rejoicing.   The yews will *smoke* no more
after such heavy snow !   On bright after-
noons, chiefly during the earlier part of
the month, it was exactly as if smouldering
fires burnt within some of them so hidden
were they in clouds of smoke.   There
must have been always a light breeze
stirring at the time ; yet the air would
mostly seem unusually still when this
smoke arose.   And then, when it cleared
off, the yews were like 'dusty millers,'
powdered over with pollen.   One or two
of the younger yews (they never flower
profusely until they are many years older)
give 'the idea' of bursting into fresh green
buds of spring all over them, at the points
of almost every twig.   Buds, however,
they are not, only mischievous imitations ;
or a sort of gall made by insects (mites).
Nothing can be discovered by pulling
these buds to pieces ; at least, after minute
examinations, we have never been able
to find the insect inside.   When the days
are warm and dry I have often worked
for an hour or so at one time, pulling off

the growths as high as I could reach all round the trees, but the result is small ; they soon come again as thick as ever.

My favourite Garrya elliptica is in beauty now, growing against the east wall of the entrance court. A soft veil of catkins enshrouds the tree from its top downwards ; each long catkin, just tinged with a rosy bloom, is delicately outlined against the dark round-leaved foliage. I can fancy the Garrya standing alone, thus softly veiled, upon the open sward—how beautiful it would be ! But if this ever happens I do not know, for in our climate it seems to need the support or shelter of a wall. I have been going round the garden in the bleak windy sunshine ; and I think our flowers of March are nearly many enough and varied enough to satisfy even *our* immoderate desires.

The straight walk in the kitchen garden never looks fairer, with all its roses, than now in the simple green and gold of daffodil clumps all the way on both sides. All sorts of daffodils are everywhere, from the large heavy headed double ones, to

the diminutive brilliant little Hoop petti-
coat, only three inches high. There is
Pulmonaria, Triteleia, and white violets
and patches of white Arabis, and primroses
just becoming plentiful. There is a long,
blue-rimmed border of Grape Hyacinth, and
another of metallic-shining Scillas. Blue
prevails indeed—blue Scilla and Chiono-
doxa, blue hepatica, blue Omphalodes.
Soon there will be deep blue gentian, beside which all other blues will pale. Dear
little cheerful-eyed Omphalodes! The
old plants have worn themselves out, but
young roots are spreading over some stones
near the Roman Walk, and flowering with
enthusiastic vigour. A charming Hungarian
lady the other day embraced it (so to
speak) with delight. She said Omphalodes verna grew wild in her native woods.
Amongst the rarer gems must be counted
Sisyrinchium grandiflorum, or better
named, Satin-flower, with its exquisitely
shaped purple bells, like hanging crocus
flowers ; and on the rounded south side
of Glorietta is a group of magnificently
fiery, scarlet anemones.

APRIL

IV

APRIL

' " Ay, there's easting in it,"
The white-haired sailor said,
As he looked on the sweep of tossing grey
And the flying flakes of snowy spray,
Wind-borne o'er the great pier-head.

' " Ay, there's easting in it,"
Said the herd, who his moor-watch kept ;
" The lambs crouch clustering under the Oak,
And last night a sound like sea-waves broke
As the wind my turf-walls swept." '

APRIL 3.—Yes, ' there's easting in it,' this
dry hard day, under the hard pitiless blue.
Day after day, a cold sun shines down
upon the parched and dusty world. The
sun shines, but there is none of the sove-
reign delight of sunshine. The sky is as
steel and brass; the grass is white with
frost morning after morning, and there has
not fallen one April shower to set the sap

running within the black bare trees and
loose the young leaves and blossoms bound
up within their hard buds. There is no
life in the fields, no balm in the air, ' nothing grows,' as the saying is. Everything
looks pinched and unhappy, and I think
no living thing enjoys the east wind,
except perhaps the skylarks. They, dear
souls, spring up and glory in the open
heaven above them. They rise quivering
and carolling up to the very gates ! Doubtless *they* in their joy are singing, ' Blow,
thou wind of God ! ' How beautiful are
the daffodils just now; and how their pure
cold yellow seems in harmony with the
freezing sunshine ! But they are none the
better for it, and never were there so
many imperfect, unaccomplished flowers
among them. One or two in every clump
come out uncomfortably green, or open
unkindly, and as if they could not make
up their minds to be either good green
leaves, or fair yellow flowers ! These unhappy ones are rather amusing, but they
are certainly very ugly : ' there's easting in
it.' The great mass of daffodils, however,

were never finer. I am comparing the
common single long-tubed daffodil (Tela-
monius plenus) with Sir Watkin. The
former would surely be thought almost the
handsomer of the two, but for Sir Watkin's
star-like corolla and erect carriage. Our
Cernuus, a new possession, is in bloom :
it seems almost too delicate for the open
border. But in the Boccage, there grows
the joy of my eyes, a lovely group of
cream-white daffodils !

The joy of daffodils is not to be forbid,
and their season is the most beautiful
of all the year ! Thus did my heart
decide this very evening as I wandered
amidst a flood of daffodils overflowing
every corner of the garden, surging over
every border, sprinkling every breadth
of green grass, in all the crystal clear-
ness of their yellow gold. The young
moon showered silver all about them, the
thrushes sang aloud their praises far
and near. Millions of daffodils joyously
blooming everywhere. Yet it is certain
that as soon as the gentians come, or the
apple-blossoms, or the hawthorn, or the

rose, I shall feel just the same, and shall say again, ' *This* is the most beautiful time of all!' So was it when crocuses, yellow, white, and purple, burst into splendour in those wintry days of March; so was it when long lines of Scylla, made the whole garden bluely beautiful. But the intense purity of these daffodils takes the fancy and holds it with a spell more powerful than the magic of all other colours. During sixteen years have the daffodils silently multiplied as they grew in the garden. In all these years the different strains have never mixed. The fine old double-flowering Telamon, still crowds broad reaches of the lawn, with intermingling groups of single long-cupped flowers; the double are still richly double, the single yet remain austerely single— unchanged, and as I believe firmly unchangeable. My favourite star-shaped short-cupped daffodils, however, go on doubling for ever. In sheltered corners there are choice collections of the rarer kinds. There is the coy Princess: Obvalaria and Leedsii, and pallid down-

cast cernuous, etc., etc. Little pumilis is
going off, after taking part in the soft
colour-chord touched by Glory of the
snow (Chionodoxia) blue Hepatica and
Sysirinchium.

On the grass in the orchard, are
wild Lent lilies, transplanted hither
from the sweet wild meadows of Derbyshire. They are modest little things,
most palely delicate in colour, their bent
heads all turned one way, south-east.
There is something peculiarly neat and
pretty in the half-opened bud, the long
tube being *fulled* round the edge as if drawn
in by a thread—a bit of Dame Nature's
neatest needlework! We are trying these
wild ones also in a garden border, but
I do not expect them ever to double.*
In the broad new border of the Boccage
and in the Fantaisie, heavily scented
jonquils flourish in perfect peace, their
deep content plainly visible, as it always is
with some flowers. 'Blue Roses' would

* In 1895, several years after this was written, the
Lent lilies from Derbyshire, planted in the border,
still remain single.—E. V. B.

give one little pleasure ; but how exquisite is the idea of a White Jonquil ! There are times when I am possessed with the wish for coloured flowers to be white.   A white Camellia japonica ! a white Chinese currant !   At this moment, however, a crowd of pure white daffodils is the desire of my heart.   In the garden of our castle in Spain there shall be a long green walk, bordered thickly on each side, under the pomegranate trees, with white and golden daffodils, both single and double.

In the orchard there is a green walk where one passes through the shimmering pink of large bushes of Chinese or Californian currant (ribes sanguineum). As yet they are only in rosy bud ; but there is something fairy-like in the extreme lightness of these interlacing branches, tipped with clustered points of pink ; it is better than when the flowers are full, for then a little green begins also to show and there is something gone from the beauty of them. Better still than the magic of this roseate mist, there is a certain sweet and silvery charm begun to spread over all the garden,

quite low on the ground, almost under
foot. The seeds may have lain there long,
first carried by the birds, perhaps. We
have never before observed this overspreading of White Violets. In every corner
where there may be any little bit of
border not dug—under trees, even niched
into the walls—in all parts of the garden
are white violets. We should not be
content with always white instead of
purple ; yet there is some kind of strange
little spell about the white, so that sometimes I am compelled to put on my
hat and hasten out into the garden, just
for a moment's look at their fresh pleasant
faces, and to inhale their scent. There is
no 'easting' in their perfume, whether
they come white or blue ! and indeed I
think these white violets must be here
'for luck ! ' It matters not if we have
to-day's chill sunlight, or if a black north-
easter blows, the silvery violet patches
shine on unheeding in serene and genial
lowliness. Ah, how ungrudgingly would
we not—if this might be—pass them on
into the grey life of one or two, to cheer

them for a space, when they sigh, 'Ay,
there's easting in it,' . . . . sighing sadly

'O for the perfect work of time ;
O for the other shore !
Where the riddles of years are read at last
And the east wind blows no more.'

Violets are very little flowers, but somehow there's much to say about them !
Under a sunny hedgerow of the Walk
meadow, blue and white violets grow together, with a third kind in which the
blue seems to run into the white ; white
violets dashed with blue or lilac. And
two or three years ago under another
quickset hedge in our lane, I scattered some
seeds of purple violets for the delight of
our village children, or for any little way-
farers in the spring. The seeds did not
seem to come up, and I forgot all about
them till the other day, when we saw, with
great satisfaction, a little boy and his big
brother happily engaged gathering dark
sweet Violets under the barren hedge, and
making them up into posies with a few
scant early daisies. I sowed many seeds

that year along our dull roadside banks—
common things that might well have
grown, and I counted on the children's
pleasure and surprise when they found
such lovely things in bloom—there were
Campanulas and Stocks and Poppies,
Snapdragons, Primroses, Foxgloves, and
yellow Broom, and Virginian Stock. But
never a plant came up, excepting just one
foxglove, whose fine spire of buds was
untimely plucked—and now the violets.

I do not know if the east wind has to
answer for our Forget-me-nots coming
red. Most of the blue is more freely mixed
with pink than usual, and one root, under
a chestnut tree near the water-course, has
fairly gone into deep crimson. If the seeds
can be saved, we might possibly get from
them a new variety. But a crimson forget-me-not would be unpoetical, and un-
real, and like the dark blue which appeared
a few years ago, interesting only as a
curiosity. There was some failure in the
seed last year, so that our *pavé of turquoise*
will not this season be quite so extensive
as usual. Brilliant and close-flowering,

E

however, as our garden Myosotis* is, the
pleasure of it never could compare with
the image—glassed I suppose in almost
every heart—of the clear quiet pool, set in
some sequestered meadow, on whose green
margin grew the blue forget-me-not. Or
of the place where it bloomed just out of
reach in the little stream among wavering
weeds, shedding starlets of heaven's blue
upon the water under the willows. Those
were the real *Vergessmeinnicht* of our youth,
and when we sat on the bank beside them,
or wet our feet in gaining difficult possession of them, we thought then upon the
dear old half-sad, half-foolish German
romance — never remembered in the
garden plots.

APRIL 13.—At last a gracious rain has
fallen. A sort of quickening thrilled at
once through all the garden, and now the
grass gives out a green answer to the
precious drops. There is to-day at the
southern end of the broad walk—in the untidy—because too full—border facing the
east, a new beautiful colour of Pæonies in

* Myosotis dissitiflora

their first young growth. I do not remember them before the rain ; now the
strong healthy stalks pushing up above the
ground are a full crimson red. The colour
is so vivid, it almost has the effect of some
strange flowers, seen from a little distance.
At the opposite end of the walk the onion
flavour of the Crown Imperials is not so
unpleasantly perceptible as it sometimes
has been. I remember it was long before
we discovered the source of the strong
odour pervading that part of the garden.
Not an onion anywhere near ; there seemed
nothing to account for it. Gerard says,
' the whole plant do savour or smell very
like a fox.' I think we may well forgive
our crown imperials their smell, however,
for the stately show they make ; and if
taste and fashion did not change with
flowers as with other things, they might
still be among the choice favourites of
spring. Ours ought to be somewhat taller,
a fine Crown Imperial should rise so high
that a little child might stand under the
yellow bells and look up into the moon-
stone circlet within ; for ' in the bottom of

each of these bells there is placed six drops
of most clear shining sweet water, in taste
like sugar.'   In another place are also
saffron-coloured crown imperials, coming
into bloom.   They are commoner and less
beautiful than the yellow.

This is the legend of the crown-imperial, or Pearl Lily.   ' Jesus walked in the
garden of Gethsemane.—And the lily we
call the crown-imperial lily, had just been
crowned.   And when all the other flowers
bowed their heads as the Saviour passed
along, she alone refused to bend, and held up
her head quite straight and stiff.   Jesus laid
His hand upon the flower and gently said,
" Lily, lily, be not so proud ! "   Ever since
the flowers of the crown-imperial have bent
down all round and have stood so, filled
with tears.'

I never dwell upon failures in the
garden : they are never many, and are
soon forgotten.   Here may be the place,
however, to record one small disappointment.   Round the stone floor of the
garden porch, we had made an outer rim
of gold and silver Thyme.   The intention

was, that with every passing step, crossing
over to the gravel, or with the sweep of
a trailing gown, should arise sweet thymy
odours on the air. But the thing did not
succeed. The gold and silver thyme all
died away before any one had enjoyed it
much. And yet perhaps, the idea is
worthy of another trial. Perhaps thyme
or wild mint might be induced to grow
upon the lawn, and in the mowing or the
treading it would smell deliciously. A
trimly shaped Rosemary in bloom, is about
as pleasant a sight as can well be seen on
an April day. The 'sweet gaping flowers'
of a bluish-grey, set not too thickly among
the dark green narrow leaves, give such
a sense of neatness ; they look so clean
and cool, that the wonder is the sweet-
smelling shrub should not be a greater
favourite. Two hundred years ago it seems
to have been planted in every garden.
Then there were gilded rosemarys, and
Rosemary of the poets, and several wild
rosemarys—all grown for physical or civil
purposes. It was used at weddings, and
funerals, and a bundle of it was a welcome

gift bestowed upon friends. Where rosemary flourishes nigh the house, there the
wife is said to rule. It is by no means for
any such reason, however, that so shapely
and fine a bush of it grows beside our
south porch ! It is because it worships the
sun, and when the sun shines the bees are
about it all day long.

> ' *The life that throbs in April's heart.*
> *Wakes every mortal thing ;*
> *And grief, with birds and buds and flowers*
> *Stirs freshly in the Spring.*'
>
> *Burns.*

M A Y

V

MAY-DAY EVE IN THE MORNING

'Well may I guess and feel
Why Autumn should be sad,
But vernal airs no sorrow feel,
Spring should be gay and glad.'—*Keble*.

THE hour from 8 to 9 A.M. is often the quietest in all the day. Everybody has gone to breakfast, and the garden is deserted. Thrushes and blackbirds are breakfasting all over the meadow, and the distant singing heard among the further elm trees gives emphasis to the nearer silence. Even the bees are gone home to breakfast; only here and there a lumbering old humble-bee grumbles alone in the blossoming fruit trees. It is time for the young nestlings' second or third meal, and the tame robin redbreast (who, though it is no longer winter, still visits the window) is hurriedly packing a slender worm in her bill, and then, by the direction of her flight

betrays the cherished secret of her treasure.
Yet it must be confessed that when the air
is less chilly the hour is often fuller of mur-
muring stir among the birds and bees than
it is to-day.

> ‘ The small bees busy at their threshold old,
> And lambs lamenting in their four-fold fold.

Cold as it is, there is one tall white Iris—just
one among a thousand budding now in
double file throughout the garden—carefully, slowly opening.   It rises above all the
other irises—first and fairest, as the first of
every flower is—and to-morrow it will be
full-blown, in honour of the day.   The eve
of May-Day should be full of mysteries in
earth and air.   A great change is approach-
ing, and all Nature knows it.   I myself but
dimly guess and feel what it may be.   It may
be that the birth of summer is at hand, and
already a few of Nature’s loveliest children
‘ haste to die.’   Snowdrops are forgotten,
and primrose-tide is fading from the woods.
Under the yellow Berberis yellow petals
lie in little heaps or lines of yellow drift :
and every pearly bud on the white cherry
trees has opened wide.   There is no wind,

but they will not last; another day or two
and the fruit will be set, and we shall see
twin cherries swelling greenly all over each
long length of blossomed bough.

Either to-day, or on May-day, one ought
to see the fairies, according to the old
Scottish legends! No fairies appeared
this time, but I saw a good deal between
eight and nine, looking from the broad
walk, upon our old kitchen garden walls,
bright with the eastern sun. How shall
the charm of these old brick walls be
described? Words could never paint it.
In the clear glow of morning light, the reds
are so delicately pure and warm, and they
are mottled with such varied greys and
many-tinted yellows. There are stout old
buttresses, too, mossed and ferny, and grey
with eld. Ancient rugged pear trees grow
up against it, and their outstretched
knotted old limbs are set now with knots of
flowers, and young, tender leaves, and the
half-transparent shadow of every flower
and leaf lies still, or trembles on the wall.
One of these pear trees, quite worn out
and decayed with age, had been cleared

away last winter, leaving a broad vacant
space, a space that is not bare, but full of
interest. Little incidents and details, un-
observed before, were plainly seen this
morning. There is a curious arrangement
of wood - bricks built in regular order
amongst the others. Worm-eaten and
decayed, they have weathered to the same
colour as the greyer of the bricks, and are
so inconspicuous as to pass usually unre-
marked. These wood-bricks must have
been devised for the more careful nailing
up of fruit trees. The fine new garden
walls of those days might not be disfigured
with nails! some have fallen out, leaving
recesses convenient for wrens' and other
nests. Suddenly appeared a curved line of
bricks, set end-wise, showing where once
had been a low-browed narrow door-way,
bricked up long since. There is another
as low and narrow, faintly visible farther
down. Carlyle wrote of the days 'when
dresses were smaller and thoughts were
larger.' Certainly our modern door-ways
are mostly wider than those of older date.

The old walls, with the sunlight dis-

covering upon them traces of Time's landmarks, are enough to set one dreaming
of those former days, and for the moment
it is easy to live in many a bygone scene ;
to fancy the precise training of the fruit
trees to the wood-blocks; the daily traffic
through that little doorway. One could
see the gardeners with their quaint old-
fashioned wheel - barrows and watering-
pots going in and out; and I recalled the
day named in Evelyn's Diary, when
George Evelyn and his cousin John
Evelyn of Sayes Court, walked through
the door together—George, showing his
gardens with due pride—John, with grave
observant eye, noting how they were
'exquisitely kept though large.' That
afternoon was July 23, 1679. The sunny
wall stood then in deep shade on this
side, and where now, on May Eve, two
centuries after, Pear blossoms whiten all
over it, George Evelyn's young trees were
ripening their first fruits. Along the top
of the wall grow wild grasses and crested
moss. There is a plant of Shepherd's
Purse with glorious spread of seed and

flower, luxuriating up there in lofty, safe
seclusion.   Seen from below, so freshly
green against the blue, these wild things
do—to us—enhance the picturesqueness
of the old wall ; and while looking up at
them thus, one feels in some degree that
curious sense of infinity, the reason of
which no one ever has explained.   The
Evelyns in their day would have treated
them as unruly weeds, and would have
made short work with them.   Not half-an-
hour hence, when the Traveller turns the
corner, and his gold face looks the other
way, the old door and the wooden bricks
with the vision of that summer day two
hundred and five years back, will fade fast
and be lost in shadow.   Another old wall
on the other side of the lawn is also
propped at intervals with heavy buttresses.
The aspect is north, and on these rude
masses of old brick grow my wild gardens.
The buttresses are gnarled and irregularly
scored and furrowed by huge ivy stems
veiled under moss and lichen.

The finest of the two ' gardens ' is that
one nearest Syringa and the greenhouse

door. There, a Nut tree of 6 inches, and a
Yew 3 inches high, are thrown into the
shade by two great Moon Daisies and a
giant Broom. These are my forest trees!
The broom don't care for so much cold
shade, and every season makes rampant
efforts to reach above it and catch the sun
upon its golden plumes. It is all but at
the top now. If I look down very closely
a miniature landscape may be discerned—
strips of flower garden inwoven with a wild
scene of mossy caves and deep ravines.
The edges of all these tiny fissures are at
this time faintly blue with eyebright of
microscopic littleness. One must almost
use a glass to see plainly the tiny perfect
flowers, no bigger than a pin's head, with
little leaves and stalks to match. Delicate
small grasses overhang the mouth of the
caverns, where small wild beasts of insect
race lie lost after their night of rapine.
Weird jungles of grey Cup-moss and lichen
skirt the garden side, and sheaves of mimic
bulrush wave gold-brown heads in a morass
of greenest moss; and then we come upon
a brilliant little daisy, every stalk a-flower

in the very perfection of blithe good
humour, though not one single ray of sunshine has ever touched its silver.   A rather
coarse Polipody fern in part supports the
daisy's roots, and one or two more tender
ferns droop gently near it.   The group is
fringed below with a lilac patch of chance-
sown aubrietia.   Perhaps a scarlet wood
strawberry will ripen late on the tufted
pink runners that are always climbing
higher up the buttress; and I shall soon
look for the pretty Draba verna, which
with one or two sister weeds—all micro-
scopically small—will in their courses
bloom and fade here through the summer;
that is, if they are not overtaken by the
drought already threatening.

Along the upper ledges young leaves of
Cymbalaria are coming thick and fast.
This lovely well-known little antirrhinum
is more or less common all over Europe,
I believe, however named — whether
Mother of Thousands, as in the old stone
fences of Somersetshire, or in Scotland
Wandering Sailor, or the Fronde della
Madonna of the rocks and carved pedi-

ments of Italy. Wherever old stone or marble is, there—with the universal pellitory — we find the sweet enrichment of our toad-flax.* Soon it will be breaking in avalanches all down the old buttress, and at close of summer a thick green curtain will have long been drawn over my small enchanted wild.

MAY 21.—To-day there is heavy rain, and the Gardener has just come in to announce the first blooming of a new Iris. A plant of pale grey iris was given to me last summer, and we have looked anxiously for its flowering. The Iris procession begins this year with the white and purple in lavish profusion. They flower together for the first time, alternately, along the line of holly hedge. The purple are too impatient usually to wait for the blooming of the white. These stand now in multitudes under the dining-room windows, and along the south-walk. Someone has compared them to the company of St

* Among the stones of 'the Roman walk' occurs another and more lovely variety. A. Pilosa, is its distinguishing name.

F

Ursula's white-robed virgins.   Our irises
begin to know that they are especial
favourites here, and their great size, and
luxuriance is bewildering.   Of course ' *they* '
would tell me it is only because their roots
have ' become established,' as they say.
Both Ensata and the Fleur-de-Lys bear
forcing well, and we have never been without either since January.   The fine broad
foliage of the fleur-de-lys was welcome,
for its masses of fresh green in winter,
when the flowering plants were brought
into the house.   The white flowers send
forth, however, when thus forced, a
fragrance that some find too powerful; as
Gerard says of lilac, 'troubling and
molesting the head in a strange manner,
with a ponticke and unacquainted savour.'

It is strange that Iris germanica, whose
scent I have sometimes known at Rome
(and notably where it grows round the
tomb of Cæcilia Metella) to make the
sweet air still more delicious, has here no
kind of scent.   A pleasant change of colour
comes, near the entrance court : it is purple
iris growing with a clump of amber-edged

yellow tulips. And still more refined and
lovely is the contrast upon a south wall,
of a large flowered mauve clematis, with
Gloire de Dijon rose and the brown
shoots of flexuosa honeysuckle intermixed
with white iris below. The tulips in the
tulip parterre are over, after a brilliant
existence of nearly four weeks. One day
they were seen to shine like lamps of
coloured fire, through the thinner spaces
of a large black Irish yew. The beautiful
effect never returned again ; it was perhaps due to some strange accident of light.
Light does often use 'lawful magic' mar-
vellously under the pure intensity of a
morning sky, or just before the sun goes
down. I have seen the Phillyreas in the
garden in the early hours, reflect back
positive blue from their dark foliage, and
there is a Persian lilac in bloom whose
colour is gorgeous at such a time. It is
absolutely dazzling. Birds, too, flash past
with colours that might vie with those of
oriental plumage. Green-finches on the
wing or among the branches are emerald-
green like real green parrots, or a titmouse

flits from tree to tree in 'azurn sheen,' as blue as any kingfisher. It is the way the sun strikes at this sweet hour. At sunset I have seen the great elms all glorious within, the straightness of their massive stems burning with a lurid glow from root to treetop behind the leaves ; and last evening when, after the rain, the sunset shone upon a cypress, a million rain-drops twinkling all over it became lustrous diamonds of the purest water, darting long rays of rainbow hues.

No springtime could ever be more perfect in its outward beautifulness than this May is, though indeed the rain and cold do somewhat spoil our full enjoyment. It must have been in a spring like this that Jean Paul wrote of 'winter painted green.' Yet there were days when the perfume of apple blossoms was borne through all the garden as balmily as if the breezes had not been ice Never were apple trees more snowily, rosily radiant. It was as beautiful as a dream to pass along underneath their flower laden branches ; and so abundant was the bloom that when it fell the petals

lay so thick upon the grass that the
thrushes tripped up and stumbled in their
haste to run through it! Lilac, too—a
more lasting pleasure—is in finer bloom
than ever I remember it. Lilacs do not
usually take the place they are worthy of
in our gardens. In former days, when
the 'Blew-pipe tree' was a novelty, they
planted it in the front ranks ; but now,
somehow, it seems always pushed out of
the way, and yet the loveliness of lilac
trees in May can be scarcely equalled,
while one feels that the first whiff of their
perfume in the garden is as the very heart
and soul of memory. Our old trees at the
back of the Broad Walk border are scarcely
seen from the garden. They cheerfully give
their beauty to the other side, overhanging the tarred paling of the potting-house
yard, and glorifying its business-like surroundings with a world of fragrant colour.
From an upper window of the house I
look down upon a distant view of this
tossing sea of lilac.

Two or three young lilac bushes were
planted a few years back in the orchard ;

they are better placed : one can enjoy
them more intimately, walk round them,
or pull down a branch to smell the lilac
cones.   But our white lilac, most refined
and loveliest of all, grows nowhere unen-
cumbered with shrubbery.

If the forest of the Fantaisie were but
half a mile round instead of half a rood, it
would be perfect. Its position gives variety,
that quality which charms as much in a
garden as does the play of expression in a
human face.   It is as if in following the
green garden ways we went ' from grave to
gay, from lively to severe.'

From the sunny masses of pink and
white Phlox repens, blue Gentian, and
narcissus poeticus, in the wildest profusion, ending in a wholly indescribable glow
of azalea mollis, the path winds along
smooth grass, and close-trimmed laurel
into the woodland shade, between great
clumps of purple iris growing among stones
and flints, over-run with stonecrop, violas,
and fumitory. Here, though so tiny that
some one the other day, took it for a child's
garden, there is something of the dim quiet

of a wood. Every wild plant that makes
its home in it is welcome ; even dande-
lions, and stellaria, and wood - sorrel
(flower of the Holy Ghost), one little flower
of which has just remembered it is Whit-
suntide, and opened its veined petals.

The bluebells nodding to each other
under this sun-chequered living green of
Spring, are fresh joy to me every morning
and every evening. I suppose wide sheets
of them, a very 'Heaven upbreaking from
the earth,' might give greater pleasure ;
but only in extent—scarcely in degree.
My 'wood' is but a little chink of heaven,
yet the delight of it is as pure as it is
small. There was a fear lest these wild
hyacinths might deteriorate in land not
poor enough to keep them humble ; that
downward curve of the slender stalk, which
is grace itself and the glory of bluebells,
seemed about to be lost in over-luxuri-
ance ; the heads of flower, bent low
enough however, after they were fully
blown. There are countless groups of
white, and blue, and pale mauve hyacinths
that once were wild, dispersed about the

borders ; but the cultivated ground seems
to give a certain fatness to leaf, and stalk,
and flower, which takes just so much off
from their perfect beauty.

Coming out of the wood, a sharp turn
to the left leads one into a fair round
green, and 'Glorietta' smiles out of the
enclosing thicket. Parrot tulips flaunt
in yellow and scarlet rags, amid purple
iris and red anemones, round one-half of
the charmed circle ; the other half, being
turned from the sun, can only boast of
late green buds. A deeper interest lies in
the junipers above the budding tulips,
for there the birds build, and know themselves secure.

JUNE

VI

THE JUNE GARDEN

*'The whispering of the boding trees
The deep-toned music of the soul.'*

*'One hour with thee, when burning June
Waves her red flag at pitch of noon;'*

JUNE is the most beautiful month in all the
year. There is nothing like it. After
years of wavering choice between autumn
and the spring—which might be best—the
decision is made, and the question, in my
own mind at least, at rest for ever, on this
green June morning. There is nothing
else on earth that ever can compare with
beautiful, flowery, flowerful June! The
colour of the leaves is exquisite, and as
perfect is the colour of the shade they cast.
After June is past it will be different, since
the leaves will no longer then be thinly
half-transparent ; but now on this glorious

1st of June, the sun shines down upon the
trees from his throne of cloudless blue, and
there is no shade ; it is all green sunshine
under the trees.   The green, when many-
tinted summer is new, if not so brilliant as
autumnal gold and red, is yet sufficiently
various to satisfy the eye.   The olive-green
of young oak, and poplar, and ash,
contrasts with the fresher greens of elm
and lime.   I remember an old Somersetshire woman, who used to say, the woods
in June were like a piece of 'lady's embroidery work.'   To-day the hedgerow
elms and lines of distant wood are lustrous.
No other word could give so well this
wonderful glow of June upon the leaves,
and only a poet could have found the
word ! *   And then when the sun is down,
and the glowing trees are by contrast dim
and solemn, and the soft 'tur-turring' of
the turtle-doves in the thorn tree in the
field is hushed, I know that I shall find the
white Irises more shining in their polished
whiteness than during all the day, filling

* 'Slides the bird o'er lustrous woodland, etc. —
Tennyson.

the air with perfume. In the garden, we
have gold as rich as October ever gave ;
and we have silver which is June's alone.
Laburnums rain gold above the golden
broom, and intermix with Silvern heaps
of white-thorn and silvery broom. And
when did ever autumnal-mellowed beech
light up the yellow groves with velvet fires,
so softly red as the young shoots of copper
beech, which scatter now their spray of
rubies and clear jacinth, dropping down
between us and the sun ? And when did
autumn ever burn with such crimsons as
glow in these scarlet double thorns, or in
the piled-up splendours of rhododendron,
which now illuminate the woods ?

The yews and yewen hedges have put
on a new face, and conceal all trace of
gloom beneath young leaves of russet-
gold. Yet there is regret and grief this
beautiful June morning ! I find myself
quoting Wordsworth, saying to myself,
'There is a change, and I am poor' ; for
the whole garden is all jubilant with song,
but the song that is best is not heard.
There is no nightingale this year. We

listen and watch in vain. Sometimes
some thrush singing notes of unwonted
fire and sweetness will for a moment deceive
the ear : this has happened once or twice.
But when indeed the nightingale sings,
he is never mistaken for a thrush. What
alas ! is the mysterious cause of our loss ?
We are fain to hope it may be the cold
winds of May and April ; because there are
no glowworms ; or because there is so little
oak about the place. (Oak scrub must this
autumn be planted somewhere.) Anything
is better to believe than the ugly reason
of bird-stealers. Whatever the reason be—

> 'Such change, and at the very door
> Of my fond heart, hath made me poor,'

Of a winter garden it is easy enough to
write. But in June ! the garden in midsummer ! Out of the fulness of it how is
choice to be made of one bright flower for
praise more than another ? It is a world of
surpassing beauty. This morning, in the
still shade of a south window, one small
petal dropped upon the window-sill from
a flowery branch of cotoneaster (*Good
Neighbour*). One is seldom present just at

the very moment when a petal falls. The
flower may wither or be shaken in the
wind, or fall at a touch, and the leaves be
scattered. But when both shape and
colour are unchanged, and yet the petals
drop quietly one by one in some profound
calm of a summer dawn or evening twilight,
there is pathos in it. The flower is not
dead, but her time has come. The flowers
of the cistus family, which are now delight-
ing us, quite literally have their day. In
the morning there is a mass of bloom; at
evening not a single flower remains. The
sole trace left is a pink or white or yellow
mosaic, where the falling petals have
showered down upon the grass or gravel.
The difficulty is, to find room enough for
cistus. They require some bank or lengths
of rock garden, to be given up entirely to
them. Then there might be a blaze of
colour through all the summer, in favour-
able weather, for they do not like too much
rain. In proportion to the brief individual
existence of the Cistus flowers are their
innumerable buds. And they are as costless
as they are lovely ; a few packets of seed

will stock a garden! Once we had the pink Riviera cistus of the large grey-green leaves and exquisite flowers which light up the hills and dusty roadsides like rose-coloured lamps alive in broad daylight! Our plants perished in some unusually severe frost. The white cistus, with narrower, more polished, aromatic foliage, is hardier, and seems quite happy here in a south aspect. We have but one old Gum Cistus, as fragile, and more wondrously beautiful than all the rest. How the folds and crumples in the satin of her ample petal do but enhance her beauty! It grows on the lawn at the foot of a Noisette rose that now envelopes the bare stem of a dead weeping ash. The rose climbed up to the top of the tree, and falls over in a great luxuriance of flower and leaf and thorn. Within the thorniest heart of this thorny rose-thicket a thrush has her nest. I think, in her wisdom, she this time made it just a little *too* safe. The young thrushes still sit full fledged in the nest; I think they dare not tempt the thorns.

As we pass through the south porch the

martin from her mud hut over the door skims out into the sunshine. When she begins to sit there will be little time for these wide sweeps of flight, or to idle upon the Rose arches, twittering and preening those long, blue-black wings of hers! On either side the porch there grows a lavender bush and a rosemary. The lavender is failing, as it did last summer. The bud-stalks look quite firm and healthy up to a certain point, and then each head hangs down and in a little while they look withered and black—as if they were strangled. 'Some failure at the root,' is the Gardener's verdict for this and many another unpleasantness in the garden. Is it not mostly 'failure at the root' in many of our mistakes outside the garden? None of the other lavender plants seem affected in the same way, fortunately. Ferns and a fine root of Turncap Lily grow at the back of the lavender, and up the porch wall is a young Banksia rose climbing apace, and flowering for the first time. It ought to have been yellow, but it has come white. Under the rosemary

G

is a great old conch shell, kept filled with
fresh water for the birds.   The narrow
border that runs along under the Oak-
room window is my trouble and my dear
delight.   I hope nothing will ever lead me
to call it a 'herbaceous border!'   It has
become so much the fashion to call everything herbaceous which is not 'bedding
out,' that the meaning of the word is
usually lost sight of, and all kinds of woody
perrenials are, so it seems to me, included
in the 'herbaceous border.'   The phrase
also seems to leave out all the poetry of
the garden.   Not, I think, more than a
dozen or fifteen years old, it dates from
the first rage for yellow calceolarias and
pyrethrums and the carpetings, when
'herbaceous' things were admitted only
somewhere out of the way by sufferance.
May this be the first and last time I
have to write 'Herbaceous border!'

Under the window a cotoneaster bears
good promise of its pink liliputian apple
crop for the blackbirds in October.   And
then there is a little wilderness of wood
strawberries.   They want to have it all

their own way here, and mean to get it.
They smother the hepaticas, and choke
the irises, and over-reach the turf verge;
and then ground-Ivy stretches along and
over the strawberries, and has to be
quickly made an end of. Red wood-straw-
berries are ripening for the children, mixed
with a few of the yellow-flowered fragaria
indica, whose berry is very handsome, but
so acrid as to ensure its stay safe enough
on its stalk. Neither child nor bird would
taste a second time. Italians, with their
characteristic gentle fun call it 'Inganna
Donna.' Vine and pomegranate and
white French honeysuckle, clematis and
Eccremocarpus, grow up in more or less of
wild luxuriance around the window. The
pomegranate never yet has flowered,
though her sister plant (since dead) in
another part of the garden used to flame
with blossom. Were it possible to decide
which to like best of all these, one or two
at least might attain perfection. It ought
perhaps to be the pomegranate, and a
clear place should be made for it. But
none of the others can be sacrificed; and

indeed I wish for a pyracantha and a
Ceanothus (for its blue), and a hundred
others, to be added.   Then there come the
Star of Bethlehem and Pink Convolvulus
and a line of stately white Lilies which
always bloom well; and just now brilliant
roses upon unpruned trees, in gadding
wreaths of beauty, stray above the strawberry leaves, with a sullen glow of yellow
and purple iris (Darius) between the
wreaths.   This tall Iris defied the over-
mastering luxuriance about their roots,
while the beautiful 'Versailles' was dis-
couraged and withdrew herself.

There is aromatic Santolina and woodruff
and Japan anemone, all mixed up, and
entangled with the wood strawberries, and
the border ends at a pink wall—pink with
great hanging bunches of the old china
rose.   Right in front, indifferent alike to
strawberries and all the world, are three
Euphorbias.   Of their own good will and
choice they grow up here.   It would be
cruel to uproot them, they stand so firm
and grand in their placid self assertion.   I
do not love them, but they compel my

regard. It has been remarked of them that they are beautiful, from the decision of character they display. Even from seed, they know how they intend to grow, and they complete their plan. There is the smooth firm stem, straight as a line, in colour emerald washed with amethyst, and the narrow leaves, exactly matched in size, placed with perfect symmetry up the stem till they reach the four-branched seed-holders, which proceed like a branching capital from the top of the green tall pillar. The seed-holders on the four branches support leaves of another shape in ordered pairs, and each pair guards a poisonous-looking flower or seed. From first to last there is not a shade of indecision in the mind of any one of these three tall euphorbias. (Caper spurge).

The 'Roman Walk' in the morning, when shadows fall, is almost picturesque. There are some large clumps of Sysirinchium striatum in profuse bloom ; the flower spikes and iris-like leaves are most 'showy,' contrasting well with the rocks and rounded masses of leaf and flower near

them.   The little pale yellow flowers,
taken singly, may seem rather insignificant,
yet there is something moving almost, in
their religious attention to the hour which
unwritten laws have determined ; for even
when gathered and kept in water in the
house, at a distance from the windows,
they shut up just the same, punctual to
a minute.   Lovely little purple Linaria
reticulata (aureo-purpurea) scatters itself,
self-sown, about the ledges, with the sweet
sad-coloured night stock ; and I am afraid
we tread heavier than need be upon the
camomile, spread flatly·on the stony walk,
to make it give out all its aroma.   The
small campanula pulla's deep purple bells,
nod in crevices near edelweiss clothed in
grey cottony bloom.   It is curious to see the
horror which an English dweller in Switzerland feels for this throned queen of alpine
flowers !   That edelweiss, a name *we* pro-
nounce almost with reverence, should
ever be called 'a cockney flower,' seems
almost past belief.   Yet so it is, and I am
sorry, for there had been a certain pride
when I thought our plants were finer on

the heights of the rock-garden, than in its lower ranges! There is mesembryanthemum and painted portulaca, a coral schizostylis, a yellow sysirinchium, and the stonecrops are coming into bloom. The artichoke rears itself grandly, almost like some grey-leaved giant fern, on the top ridge of rock, casting a great shadow across the stones.

A broad border—screened from a stray bit of kitchen garden by a battlemented arbor-vitæ hedge—has been divided into large squares of favourite plants. There is a square of ranunculus, and this is a disappointment. I believe the flower resents its removal from the old place under the south wall. Our ranunculus used to be small fireballs of vermillion and gold. Then there is a square of yellow sweet sultan, and with it a lovely lily with sea-green silvery leaves. Pancratium maritimum is the right name, I believe, but I prefer to call it a Star Lily. There are carnations, and then most delicately beautiful Spanish iris; a large flowered variety. The last square in the border is a blue mass of anchusa, not Italica, but the native wild sort.

The air just there is perfumed with musk. We let the musk wander at will all over this border. We give it neither care nor culture, and it gives back to us, for nothing, the treasure of its sweetness. With the parterre which lights up the lawn before the dining-room windows, I have little to do. The Gardener plans the colours and arrangement of it, and I feel it is in good hands ; two centre beds this season appear to me especially happy. They are the white Bride gladiolus, mixed with deep red Tuscan rose; pure white and crimson.

The other long-shaped, narrow parterre we have tried to pattern out like one I saw last summer on a sunny Somerset rectory terrace. It was in vandykes of many-coloured verbena ; ours is chiefly variegated and scarlet pelargonium, blue lobelias, both bronze, leaved and green, dwarf ageratum—tagetes, for yellow, and serastium tomentosum, known sometimes as Summer Snow. This snow looks very brilliant from a distance, seen through openings in the dark yew hedge. White

is perhaps too much neglected in the
ordering of coloured plots ; yet in all the
best art of old times, in stained glass or
eastern embroideries, it is the white parts
that give brilliance to the whole.   In the
garden, yellow is the trouble.   calceolarias
I will not have ; I seek vainly some low-
growing yellow, the same tone as the little
double yellow rose that is teasing me by
blooming high up out of reach by the
garden gate.   It should have the same
effect, only in yellow, as the pink silene.

A short time since this Silene was used at
Cliveden in a way that once seen, cannot
be forgotten.   An immense circle of pink,
lay like a magic ring upon the grass.
There is a set of jewel-shaped beds on a
grand scale, leading up to it on either side.
Between the ring and the lofty terrace,
and the house, there simply lies unrolled,
about a quarter of a mile of green velvet.
Beyond the pink ring, dip down in sweetly
wooded lines, steep cliffs and banks, to
level meads, and windings of the silver
Thames.

JUNE 24.—On this midsummer morn St John's wort, under the Elms, is not yet in bloom. Yet I thought as I went over the garden, there could not be a more ideal 24th of June.

White and purple foxglove throng together in stately beauty in the Boccage and Fantaisie, with heads bent in the midday sun : but where one slender spike— milk-white or red—rises alone in some shady spot, peering through green brake fern, that, is better still! I wonder what like was the 'lesser dusky foxglove, observed by Gerard in John Tradescant's garden. Also his 'Digitalis ferruginea, with flower the colour of iron.' A fine plant of the yellow Swiss foxglove lives snug and solitary, under a currant bush in the kitchen garden. It is certainly handsome, but I never know whether to admire it much or not. There is always an uncertainty about the name of foxglove. In old French it is *Gante nostre dame ;* in high Dutch, as in German, *Finger-hut.*

And Roses !—It is roses, roses everywhere. A very Pasque della Rose. Never

do I remember the garden to be so much
of a real rose garden ; and the sweetest
rose of all is that which decks the sweet
brier hedge. Paul Nèron, with all his
seven inches across and no scent, is nothing to that little deep-pink brier rose !
The damask roses overspreading a corner
at the south wall are an ideal of rose loveliness. It is worth while to make a good
south place for this old rose ; it will soon
repay you a hundredfold in delicious
beauty. Once more, after nigh two score
years, I have the pleasure of smelling a
York and Lancaster rose. Her perfume
is divine. And we have a real black rose
(Empereur de Maroque ?), if gathered before the sun has time to burn it, most
beautiful—haunting the memory with that
old foolish rhyme—

> ' Rosy in the parlour, Rosy in the hall :
> Rosy was a black Rose, better than them all.'

As for our old blush rose, age does but
increase its charm.

JULY

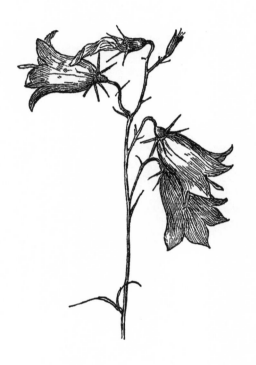

VII

JULY

'This too will pass.'—*Persian Saying.*

JULY 3.—The thought of June Roses would
have been marred had the grievous blight
that fell upon some of them been spoken
of at the time. Happily ours, which are
affected thus, are few, and the disfigure-
ment they suffer, slight compared with the
reports from other places. The roses
most dear to me have, however, suffered
most. The leaves of the Damask roses,
filling up that corner of the old south wall,
are white with blight ; some of the York
and Lancasters the same, and the leaves
of some few other kinds are spotted all
over with brown. Not one of the Tea
roses is touched, nor any of our new
roses. Where the green leaves are

affected the flowers themselves also suffer,
and look pale and stunted. Far worse
than blight are the ravages of that cruel
caterpillar which skins the leaves. He
seems to prefer the old Blush rose to all
others, and its leaves are the first to be
attacked. I confess I hate the skinner,
and destroy as many as I can lay my
finger on. He is as wily as he is destruc-
tive, and being the same colour as the leaf
is very hard to find. He has a way of
lying close along the very edge of a leaf,
or stretched out in such a position as to
be almost indistinguishable from the veins.
At mid-day, when the skinner has turned
in under the leaf for shade, it is useless
to hunt for he cannot possibly be seen.
The best time for a successful massacre
is in the morning, as early as you please.
A little patch of fresher colour betrays a
fresh-skinned portion of a leaf; there the
enemy lies, invisible, except to the long-
practised eye. As soon as he is discovered
turn the leaf over and squeeze him tight ;
there are grounds, however, for a dismal
suspicion that unless the head be crushed

the creature refills himself, the skin being
tough, and next day he is at work again as
hungry as ever. This suspected occurrence,
however, I refrain from too closely verify-
ing. The rose pest of former years—that
little bright green caterpillar who after
awhile sewed himself up in a leaf, became
a tiny black chrysalis, and then emerged a
smart little yellow moth, was not nearly
so bad as the voracious Skinner. It is long
since that little moth used to be too
common in the garden. To see it again
would at once bring back the past, with
a feeling of dark summer evenings in
long-lost years, and a pervading sense of
the smell of rain upon the summer leaves.

There are some insects which would
seem to be less abundant now than formerly.
It gave me pleasure to meet a cockchafer
one morning! The burnished rose-beetle
who used to sit like a green jewel in the
heart of a rose, or burr over the roses in
the sunshine, I never see here now. Even
the little leaf cutter bee has deserted us.
His neatly rounded cuttings, sawn out of
the rose leaves, disfigured them infinitely

H

less than one day's work of a skinner!
The musk rose that we planted last year is
flowering freely; small flowers with a small
delicious scent. I wonder if the delicate pink
of its petals is the ' musk-colour ' of some
old writers! Does not Shakespeare write
somewhere of a ' musk-coloured coat? '

The white noisettes climbing all over
our old Stone Pine droop down to
the very grass in trails and wreaths
covered thick with bunches of little
white roses in lavish beauty. The curious strong fragrance fills all that end of
the garden. A child, a little elf of blue
eyes and pink cheeks running here and
there through and through the rose-falls,
was one day, like a vision from fairyland!
Rosa microphylla has grown herself into a
great green bush in the Fantaisie. But as
to flowering, she seems to think little of
that : two or three red flowers only, of no
account. The darlings of the year are the
great broad-flowered York and Lancasters.
I count them over morning after morning
as a miser counts his gold. It is worth a
visit just after sun-rise to see and smell

them with the dew upon their petals.
They are what Chaucer would call ' brode
roses,' so wide do their firm and well-set
petals spread. The white Cabbage—which
survives in borders skirting the older,
more distant shrubberies—is this summer
more than ever bounteous in its pure
white bloom. White Roses, however,
are not my favourites, excepting perhaps
Niphetos, the waxen Devoniensis and the
Japanese Rosa Rugosa.

There are summer days when it is too
hot for any but white flowers 'to deck the
house,' and in such sultry heat white
roses help to cool the shaded room. A
rose-de-meaux, a little perfumed nest of
prim pinkness, has bloomed like an old-
fashioned woodcut under the holly hedge.
I want to have near it the tiny Fairy rose
of former years, a wee bush pinked over
with the wee-est of China roses. Several
new plants of Souvenir d'un ami are
blooming well. No rose lasts so long
when gathered, as this does. The old
Maréchal Niel in the greenhouse has re-
newed his youth, and has given us his

hundreds this spring, while one planted under a north wall (according to advice) failed to do better for us than give a few greenish buds. The roses of the Boccage are superb in size and colour. The new ground suits them, and for half the day they are shaded by the elms. For a modern rose, I like Beauty of Waltham as well as any ; its form and luminous colour, emitting rays of crimson that almost ' bid the rash gazer wipe his eye,' are as perfect as any such rose can be. In the shade, behind the others, modestly blooms a lovely new rose, Madame Audot, scarcely differing, however, from our old friend the Maiden's Blush—perhaps a little richer in colour, and in scent a little poorer. It is pleasant to come suddenly upon this blaze of roses at a distance from the house, and divided from the nearer pleasaunce by grassy paths and lines of trees. So much for our Rose garden.   .   .   .

The garden is more fragrant this summer even than is its wont. One cannot tell which sweet scent does most prevail, whether that of sweet peas, or mignonette,

or honey-scented Alyssum; while about the iron gates in the old brick walls flexuosa honeysuckle flings perfume far and near. The sweet pea hedge round half the tennis-lawn is full of lovely caprices of colour. One set of white blossoms is tinged with pale bluish. That quaint, patchy, grayish and white kind, which by some absurd association of ideas, reminds me always of the old sign of the 'Bald-faced Stag' on Putney Heath, is frequent, and so is the old fashionedst of all —the pretty pink and white. We have not yet the new pink sweet pea, the colour of a moss rose or of raspberry cream. Plain white is, after all, the best perhaps. Nature never planned a lovelier flower of such airy lightness. It might shake its butterfly wings and fly, it is so lightly poised upon the slender stalk! Perhaps to the name 'sweet pea,' and to the sweet freshness of the flower, memories of childhood cling more closely than to any other garden name.

Sweet peas and mignonette should always grow together. Even the down-

trodden Everlasting pea ('Pease everlasting,' and 'Save euerlasting,' as Gerard
calls them), with its large frank blossoms,
has this year won its way to favour.
That plant is in itself an epitome of all
the sermons of the year, with Courage
and Constancy for their text! It is as
good as a meditation by Jeremy Taylor.
We were very grave about it last year;
only a *very little* was to be permitted; it
was denounced as too encroaching; and a
quantity of it was ruthlessly cut away.
We believed its humiliation to be secure.
Not a bit of it! Never did it spread and
flourish and flower more abundantly than
it has done this summer. It ran round
the corner of the house and made a blooming bower of itself in the shade under the
east porch. It gave a rich deep pink
background for the white irises, and Blush
roses to the south; it actually climbed
up and looked in at the dining-room
windows, and nodded to us as we sat at
breakfast. 'J'y suis et j'y reste!' it said,
as plain as words; and after all I had
to confess its conquering beauty. The

Gardener would say I am rather weak about some things. 'pease everlasting,' has overcome ; and so has the white briony. I had said that this briony should not advance beyond a certain point. And I found myself to-day surrounded by the beauty of ten thousand ice-green blossoms, overspreading a low ivy wall, at least twelve feet beyond the bounds I had set. With unnumbered lengths of out-shot tendrils stretching all over it every way in eager quest for the touch of some sympathetic branch, with glossy ivy and blue berberis berries mixing through the flowers and foliage, it is certainly as people say, 'a picture.'

Near a little wicket gate at the end of a grass walk, grows a female briony, smaller and more reticent, wreathed about with round green fruit. During a short absence this was written to me—'No one has passed through the little green gate since you left, I am sure ; the briony has put out a tiny hand which clasps it so tight.' Totally different and most charming in its way, are the clumps of Alströmeria, whose orange blossoms pass 'wrapt through many a rosy change' into pink and white. It is invaluable in nosegays for the flower-glasses. It will have to be transplanted from its rather obscure corner at a distance from the house by the garden-men's cottage. It would keep the east border 'furnished' until the time of phloxes. Ever since mid-winter, the flower-glasses on our tables have glowed with a rich succession of Amaryllis formosissima and double scarlet hibiscus. The long firm petals of this amaryllis, well named 'the most beautiful,' burn red beneath the silken surface—a just imitation of old red enamel. I never tired of watching the play of inner light ; the turn of each petal shone like a piece of old jeweller's work.

JULY 24.—One month has passed since the garden lay flushed with the full glory of midsummer. It is a little sad that nothing now remains but a memory of it ; that thinking of the garden flowers one must say that this, and this, *has been !* Many a flower since June has budded, bloomed, and fallen ; and like the quickly passing sweetness of them, many a friend has come and gone. The dry, green paths hedged in with beech or rose are haunted in this parching weather, not alone by waving shadows on the grass, but by dear memories of a face or a voice that was here, and is not. The garden, through all its prime, was remarkable for its blue. Cloudy pillars of delphinium rose everywhere on the borders, showing well especially among the cryptomerias of the Fantaisie. There were many shades of blue, from pale sky to ultramarine. The dark blue double kind is a desirable plant, for its quality of lasting longer than its single sisters. Within the walls there grew a lovely group of white lily with pink roses against a misty background of blue larkspur, while on the other side the walk reigned in brilliant confusion, Himalayan poppies of every red and rosy tint. People say that these poppies, which we call Himalayan, or annual poppies, are common. Yet nobody seems to grow them ! They have been from May till now—to ourselves and every visitor—the wonder and joy of the garden. Whether double or single, like the field poppy they are full of a happy radiancy of colour which cheers both eyes and heart.

New combinations of colour and pattern are perpetually coming ; and I do not despair of the scarlets some day running into pure orange-yellow. There is a low-growing double kind, scarcely distinguishable from a pink carnation. There is one half-double with white petals hemmed with pink, and one streaked with crimson. The colours are all bright and clean, set off by the yellow stamens. One or two are rather handsome with black centres ; but these have none of the clear joyous grace of my favourites. For ' decking the house ' (to use again Parkinson's quaint phrase), they are admirable, lasting fresh for days, if gathered in the cool of morning. To me the petals are like fairy shells ; my housekeeper is reminded by them of the muslin gowns her grandmother used to wear.* The whole race of

* Our Himalayan poppies, having bloomed with

French poppies, so called, are far inferior, despite their grand seed vessels, and their fine grey foliage. . . . I am rebuked by the sweet face of one of these very poppies looking reproachfully at me across the table. The colour is vermillion-red and white, most delicate and pure. The seed of that poppy must be marked.

In the white splendour of their contrast to the poppies, how beautiful the blooming of Madonna lilies has been! (it is all 'has been,' now!) Does any one know why the lily *leaves* almost always fail? Before their buds flowered our lilies for the most part looked deplorable—their withered leaves hanging down around the tall stems. In due time, when the stems were crowned with the majesty beside which the glory of Solomon was as nought, we forgot the dreary deadness of the foliage. In Switzerland, where the cottage gardens are filled like those in England, with white lilies, I am told the stalk-leaves remain green. Two or three of our finest

us since 1872, have since become known as 'The Shirley Poppy!'

clumps failed suddenly—in one night, it seemed—the doomed plant withering down to the very bulb. This was an unusual disaster, and I blamed 'the invisible worm that flies in the dark and howling storm.' In the same border we have several great plants of Lilium auratum without a speck upon their leaves.

The Evening primrose (Œnothera) came into bloom before its appointed time, and her fair flowers are even larger than usual. Downy-winged moths hover round them in the dark warm evenings. It is said that those who watch may see the buds open. I have watched, but had never patience to wait long enough. Most flowers are best in the morning, when they are refreshed with dews and darkness ; but to see Œnothera aright she 'must be visited by the pale moonlight,' when the air is still and heavy with the odours of night-scented flowers under the full golden moon of July. On such a dewless night, Œnothera expands her broad primrose flowers, and seems to throb through all her being with a strange moon-life. Once sown, the evening primrose takes care of itself ever after. We have them growing in a line along the Larch walk, all twined about and dressed with a large-blossomed wreathing pink convolvulus. Another company of them edging an evergreen border shine in the light of loveliness out of the sombre brown of cryptomerian darkness. Alas! Œnothera owns one fatal flaw. It is hard even to whisper of its repulsive smell—a smell which is also so sensitive that the flower seems to give it out or retain it at will. At night, if the stem be shaken, or if the flower-cup trembles at the touch of a moth as it alights, out pours the dreadful odour. I shall hope some day, for the perfumed white variety. Another old love of former years is the Indian moonflower. Some of the large white seeds were sent us in the winter from Madras, and now I am anxiously watching the growth of two fine plants which sprung from them. It used to blow at the end of July, when the moon was full, between 9 and 10 at night; opening wide, like a pure white convolvulus, with a delicious scent.

Night-blowing flowers are mostly pale
or white. The nicotiana hanging on its
stalk half-dead by day, is radiant as a
silver star when night draws on. In the
Boccage we have two fine clumps of
spiderwort (Tradescantia), a flower I remember set amongst childhood's wonders,
earliest almost of all flowers. Buds mass
themselves in clusters all over the plants,
and every day on each cluster appears a
new three-cornered purple gem. The old
fanciful likeness to spiders' legs can be
but barely traced in the leaves. There is
a sense of mysterious awe, in the way
Gerard says the leaves are good ' for the
bite of that Great Spider,' without naming
the creature more particularly.

John Tradescant lived once at Dorney
Court, not far from here. There is some
tradition that there he presented his
Pine-apple* to Charles II, and it is
not many years since a little wayside
public-house near, retained still the sign

* The first grown in England. At Dorney Court
there is an old engraving, which represents Tradescant
kneeling before the King in a garden, presenting his
pine-apple.

of a Pine-apple. 'Deborah's' little mount in the parterre was a while ago parcel-gilt with the silver of small white hare-bells, and the gold of yellow stonecrop. It is grieving to recall thus the garden as it was! Sweet things do still remain, but after all the daily waterings—sometimes whole days are spent in watering—the place as a whole is parched up with long drought. Some things dwindle, and cannot by any means be saved. Eleven weeks without rain! Long weeks when the sun burns unclouded, and the only clouds are clouds of greenfly, that is the worst; greenfly that destroy whole rows of sweet peas in a single night, and blackfly that smother the fruit trees, and distort the stalks of lovely poppies. If one sits in the garden they settle all over one, and outside the garden, down along the roads, one encounters storms of flying aphides. Flycatchers sit stupidly on the rose arches, bewildered by the myriads that float in the air. The lime avenue is dried up, and yet dripping with honeydew. Rain will come at last, however, and meanwhile the trees will ripen their wood, and it may be that good will fall rather than harm, even to the green things that claim our pity now.

I

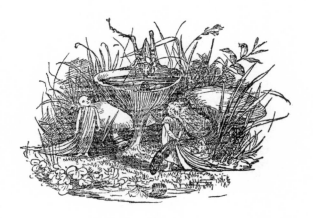

AUGUST

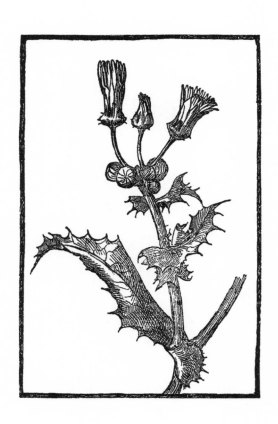

VIII

AUGUST

' Such virtue have my marigolds,
  Within their stalks enfolde,
That Phœbus with his burning beames
  Cannot their leaves unfolde.

' The double daisies all in rankes
  About my garden goe,
With comelie course of camamile
  That spreadeth to and fro.'

Hugh Plat, 1572.

AUGUST 18.—How full of charm is the
return after absence to a beloved garden!
One comes home rejoicing, to see with a
fresh eye each dear tree and each familiar
spot of lawn or border, and bringing home
stores of pleasant memories with sweet
suggestions for new delights to perfect and
bring to pass and make one's own another
day.

I note for special use these :—A Mande-

villia growing in the open air. It covers
half the front of an old house, climbing up
to the roof, and when I saw it the pure
white blossoms were clustered thickly all
over it. The situation in which this
Mandevillia grows and has flourished for
many years is warm and sheltered, the
house-walls of hummel-stone, being built
in a niche under a limestone cliff. Possibly this may not be the only greenhouse
creeper that might thrive in the open air,
at least during the summer months. We
have tried successfully the white and the
salmon-coloured black-eyed Thunbergia ;
also convolvulus from Indian seed, which
has richer and more varied colouring than
the common convolvulus major.

The lightness and gaiety of a flowery
hedge of it is indescribable. That which
I saw is nearly 10 feet high, the frame-
work made of crossed stakes, the convolvulus climbing and twining up to the top
and flowering profusely on both sides.

Espaliers of gooseberries I also saw
at an old place in Hampshire, bordering
the walks round three sides of the kitchen-

garden. Nothing can be more neat and useful than these espaliers, the gooseberries being easily gathered without much prickling by thorns, while nets fall comfortably over, protecting them from the birds. It was a delightful garden ! A long green walk lay between rows of hollyhocks, pink, black, white, and pale primrose. These lovely hollyhocks had the free, aspiring form, that is now so rarely seen when the blossoms seem to clump irregularly up the slender stem. Roses and most of the summer flowers had faded from the borders at the time of my visit. White everlasting pea—and red, strongly scented, fraxinella were among the few that still bloomed in beauty. A favourite plant of red fraxinella was lost from our garden a year or two ago, and I had not seen one since. The scent of the flower is said to be due to the emission of a vapour that can be set on fire with a lighted match. That, must one day be tried. One has but to pass a glove lightly across the flower, however, and it is perfumed all over. In another part of that old garden grew white strawberries of a peculiar kind. They flower and fruit at the same time, and the fruit, which is in flavour like a Hautbois, goes on ripening as late as October or November. Every little runner bears its flowers and strawberries. A basketful of ripe berries was gathered the day that I was there—August 10. I believe in Shakespeare's time strawberries were still called 'straeberries,' from the Saxon 'strae' or 'stray,' indicating the habit of the strawberry in putting forth runners to a distance from the parent plant, giving to both independent life. In some outland country places they still talk of the 'straeberry.'

In a beautiful sea garden, high above the sea, half hid in groves of ilex, a spot so sheltered that even in winter the lawns are scarcely ever swept by the wild sea winds, I found the little white sweet-scented* orchis in the middle of the month, growing on the brown parched-up turf. There had been no rain there, nor hardly any dew ; the lawns, destitute of any poor vestiges of verdure, lay 'gasp-

* Commonly called ' Lady's tresses,' or ' traces.'

ing as a thirsty land.' Yet here and there, made bold by the idleness of scythe and mowers, suddenly arose these green and white points of orchis. One of them, as it seemed in one night, shot up 4 inches, and this one I took home with me. It is set in water by my window, and now I can watch the untwisting of the plaited tress, as day by day its smoothness roughens with twin - petalled moonlight - coloured flowers. It was a pretty notion to liken the little flower-spike to tresses of the Virgin's hair, though one may perhaps just fancifully trace in it a mingling of pagan fairyism ; for mermaidens combed their sea-green locks, and I myself once knew the traditional fairy lady of a well, all in green, with long green hair. Her well-spring bubbled up by the side of a deep West Country lane, and many children and old people have seen the green fairy rise at twilight from the water !

The House,* whose high windows and turrets look down over these brown lawns

* Highcliff, Hampshire. Belonged at that time to Louisa, Lady Waterford.

and flowers, and ilex woods, is romantic ;
like a poet's dream, rather than a house
of the nineteenth century. Its stones,
however, are the grey stones of an old
house in Normandy. They were brought
over many years ago, and rebuilt here on
the edge of the sea in strange architecture,
with the carved mouldings and gargoyles,
and oriel windows of the past, put in just
as they were. The open parapet round
the roof reads thus in stone letters :—
' *Suave mari magno turbantibus æquora
ventis Terra magnum alterius spectare lab-
orem.*' The words seem to make music
with the soft measure of the waves below,
and the sound of the wandering winds.
The thick-leaved ilexes soon loose themselves in woods of chestnut and fir, and
paths cut through them in lines of endless
shade close in at last, each with an arch
of sapphire sea. Beyond the edges of the
woods, wild honeysuckle and low sea-
blown oaks, and brambles, grow together
in a sweet entanglement, and grassy paths
between are set with purple heather and
knapweed (knops, or hardheads), and

yellow Fleabane; and here a legion of butterflies perpetually dance and play, and make merry in the sunny weather. It should make amends for much sorrow in the world of Nature to see these thousands of beautiful creatures, secure and happy in their innocent joy.

Along this green glade your feet are every moment ensnared by long-reaching brambles, and every step disperses a fluttering cloud of butterflies. They are so tame that scarcely will they rise at your approach, often giving the observer time to stoop and examine with a lens their spangled wings and silver-topped antennæ and busy proboscis. The Fleabane is the butterflies' dear delight. (Did not the child who called them 'flutterbyes' hit upon a better name?) Two or three of diverse kinds will often prank their wings, and unrolling long black tongues, dig for honey settled together on the same flower, though flowers may not be few; but when a Painted lady (Vanessa cardui), and a silver-spotted Fritillary meet on one flower they are sure to fall out, and rising chase each other hotly. Besides the multitudes, of common and uncommon white butter-flies and little cloudlets of the azure-winged Alexis, Peacocks, and Tortoiseshells, and Painted ladies in troops with now and then a rarer clouded yellow Colias, or rapid Fritillary, disport themselves up and down the glade till past mid-day. Long may their happy world be unknown to green gauze nets and murderous ammonia bottles! I am curious to know if any variation has ever been observed in the markings of the wings of these insects. I have for years closely examined Peacocks and Tortoise-shells and Atalantas, and can never find the colours or patterns to vary in the least degree from those of the oldest specimens I can remember. In the glade dragon-flies dart fiercely to and fro, and wild ' bees are busy on their threshold old.' The honey gathered on that Hampshire coast is crystal pale this summer. It was made, as I was told, from fruit tree blossoms in the spring, the long-continued drought having dried up every drop of honey in the heather-bells.

Magnolia Grandiflora

IX
HOME AGAIN!

'Nature always wears the colours of the spirit.'

AND now I have been tasting the
pleasures of roaming through my own
principality once more!—noting with the
keenest zest the changes that eighteen
days have wrought.   I want to go all
over it again.   In a grand red glow,
covering an area of 462 square feet
of lawn, lighting up the old hall and
the windows of other rooms that look
that way, like the reflex of some fine
sunrise, just beyond the south porch, lies
the Sumach tree (Rhus cotinus).   I cannot say that it stands upon the lawn,
as would be said of any other tree, for
the beautiful soft masses of it are like
nothing else but those great white cumuli,
or summer storm-clouds, steeped in a
crimson after-glow, when we watch their
changeless glory moving slowly on, upon
the low horizon.   These sumach snows
however, are reddened by hot weeks of

July suns; they cover all the tree, till gently they shimmer down and lie still upon the turf. Not a branch or a twig, scarcely even one green leaf, strays out amid the lightness of these plumes of marabout to break their dim monotony. This plumage of the tree is sunny red, cooled with grey or lilac shadows. Ever since June has it been ripening into this miracle of misty beauty. The lawns are burnt, but the parterre is formal and brilliant just as it should be. So are the zig-zags of verbena and Pelargoniums beyond the yew hedges. The southern wall is fragrantly overhung with festooned clematis. But all these are quickly passed by. I long to know all's well with the Fantaisie and the Boccage. Ah! the sweet pea hedge round the tennis-lawn is gone and past. Turn-cap Lilies, proudly splendid, replace the roses of the Fantaisie. The cryptomeria elegans, intermingling here with verdure of wonderful freshness, seem to rejoice in the dry weather, and fair flowers of deep blue salvia begin to blow.

Three paces through the deep shadow
of 'the wood,' and there is the broad
border of the Boccage in all its glory! To
know how this had fared in my absence,
while yet the ground had not received
comfort from any kindly rain, had been
my secret trouble. I should like for the
moment to be some one else, and as a
stranger to describe this border quite im-
partially! Yet the only words I can devise
as some one else's first impression seem
cold and dry. Such as 'a beautiful band
of flowers, that reflects the highest credit
on the care and skill which have made it
what it is.' That will not do. I must be
myself, and try to give some faint outline
of it. When I saw it last—last month—
roses and pinks were over; and besides
some budding corn-flags and hyacinthus
candicans, there was little to give grace to
the border, saving certain patches and
rounds and clumps of green traced in
and out between the roses. I returned
to find this young green grown out of
all knowledge, and flowering with a strange
luxuriance of bloom, the flowers all mixing

in delicious confusion. There is Ladies' Pincushion (Saudades), made in pale coral, passing through velvet shades of red to deep 'murrey,' stuck with silver pins as usual. Lobelia fulgens (the Cardinal's flower), burn between the tufts of white and lilac Sultan's flower (Sweet Sultan). Gaillardia picta Lorenziana mingles with Gailliardia picta flowering in gold and crimson petals, fantastically nicked, set round in little coronets; a bunch or two of lilac Catananche, deep lengths of Marvel of Peru in three bright colours, many coloured China asters, double stocks, lupins, dwarf phloxes, one choice corner filled in with salpiglossis of richly varied colours, brown, purple, and grey. Sword lilies flash scarlet here and there amid all these, and grandest of all are the fine plants of hyacinthus candicans, each plant sending up three or four great stems, blue-green with the bloom of health, and each bearing a ring of bells in ivory-white. A white 'Peach-leaf bell flower,' (campanula) in a shadowy place near at hand betrays by contrast the only failure amid the perfect

K

beauty of these fine hyacinthus flowers—
failure in the purity of their whiteness.

Against a low beech hedge at the back
there is a stately line of auratum lilies,
counting seventy-three great heads of
bloom with store of buds rich in promise
for weeks far into the autumn. And
around the lilies are enlaced large African
marigolds of lemon and deep gold colour,
with scattered posies of little striped
French marigolds and of Zinnia Haageana.
At the farthest end a thicket of dianthus
superbus scents half the garden, and nearest
to the Fantaisie, a narrow grass walk in-
tersecting the border and leading into
Glorietta is fringed with lobelia sene-
cioides luxuriantly green, and most delicately blue. Chrysanthemum tricolor fills
up the corner, and on the other side deep
purple and blue perennial-blooming pansies
set off the clean yellow rays and chocolate
eyes of Rudbeckia Newmannia. Towering
above the junipers tall 'flowers of the
Sun' keep watch, their green buds not
opened yet. Mignonette and honied alyssum and orange and red tigridias seem to

grow naturally in and out between the other plants, with now and then a sharp gleam of roses in second bloom. How obscure and dull is the thought-picture, the best I can make of the Boccage border! Old Parkinson would paint it in a dozen words! He would just say, 'the place is like a piece of tapestry of many glorious colours to increase every one's delight.' Yet the colour is not all. A pervading perfume works like a charm about the place to bind in one sweet whole the outward brightness of the flowers, and the unseen soul of them, which is their scent.

I wonder how many moles there may be in the garden. The Gardener certainly would borrow Keats's phrase, and echo heartily 'the demon mole!' For they burrow and throw up their earthworks, and overturn stones, and uproot precious plants, caring nothing for right or wrong. For me, the mole is simply 'the four-handed mole,' the odd little persecuted wild beast (one of the last left in England), the little velvet-coated gentleman-navvy, who excavates in darkness, carrying his

subways across our neatest turf-walks without the least regard to propriety or order
in the garden. At the entrance of the
Fantaisie, indeed, for the last twelve years
a mole-run has existed across the path.
Our attempts to stop this right of way
have signally failed. Scores of moles were
caught year after year, and gibbeted near
the spot as a warning, till at last the
order came for executions to cease. I
could no longer endure the piteous sight
of the beautiful mole-skin coat squeezed
round the middle, and the two ungainly
serviceable hands that had worked so
hard, helplessly spread on either side. So
the underground ' taupies'' pertinacity
scored that time ! and the run remains to
this day. Long ago, when the world was
young, mole-hills were thought to be
useful for lambs to sit upon, or to shelter
under if the wind blew cold. ('Nootie-
stumps,' they call them in Gloucestershire.)
Lately, however, it has been discovered
that ' there is nothing more useful to the
floriculturist, whether for pots or borders,
than earth from a mole-hill ; ' for, ' as the

mole lives entirely on worms and insect
larvæ which are found in the best soil, that
which he throws to the surface while in
pursuit of his prey, finely pulverised, and
free from the seeds of weeds as it will be
found to be, is just in the state for producing the best flowers.'

A long-desired white Tigridia has just
now for me all the charm of a new
possession. The cream-white flowers,
with crimson-spotted centres, are a most
exquisite delight. It is one of those
strange beings which look as if they had
come from another world. Until now,
the two tigridias — the yellow and the
red with their threefold flowers—seemed
always incomplete. Now, nothing more
is needed. I do not want a blue or a
pink tigridia ; this mysterious white third
is enough.

SEPTEMBER

X

SEPTEMBER

‘ All tendrils green of every form and hue,
Together intertwined and trammell’d fresh :
The vine of glossy sprout ; the ivy mesh,
Shading its Ethiop berries ; and woodbine,
Of velvet leaves and bugle-blooms divine ;
Convolvus in streaked vases flush ;
The creeper, mellowing for an autumn blush,
And virgin’s bower, trailing airily ;—

J. Keats.

SEPTEMBER 1.—The soft triumph of the Sumach is over. According to the supreme beauty of her prime, is now her forlorn and wretched ruin. All in a day, so it seemed, the feathery fluff began to crisp and loosen. One night the west wind blew in his strength, and left our Wig tree well-nigh bald. The marabout plumes, blown hither and thither, accumulated in angles of the house, and all the borders thereabouts were bedded deep in fluffy pink. But even this relic of grace is past, and the tree, nearly un-leaved (for her feathers left no room for leaf), all dishevelled and hung with rags and tatters, is an almost ghastly sarcasm on her summer self.

SUNDAY, SEPTEMBER 13.—Autumn or spring ! 'I know not which is sweetest, no, not I'—the deep mellow calm of an evening such as this, in the middle of September, or the green brilliance of the spring. The tone is rich, like the colour of an old Venetian master; and how sad ! with the strange sweet sadness of all last things—last days, last hours. The air is filled with a golden warmth, and all tremulous with the sound of bells. The chimes of four churches make music to-gether, within a half circle of four miles. Save for the dazzling glow of tall crimson phloxes, or where the leaf of some Virginian vine, impatient of the lingering summer breaks into sudden scarlet, or where great Sunflowers burn in fair majesty serene, the

tones of colouring are subdued and solemn;
the young moon alone shines coldly through
thin saffron clouds that pass across the far
azure of the southern sky, while in the
west a pink flush, deepening into orange
fires, reflects back rosy-gold upon the
lulled earth beneath. Across the petunias
and many-coloured zinnias * bend fruitful
branches of apple and of pear. There is a
sense of settled calm and peace, of home,
and of all that may be most pleasureful and
most secure, in these plenteous boughs
weighed down by the load of their good,
great apples, and gently swelling pears,
and the mellow round of each ripening fruit
glows as if illumined from within. And
now a great silence steals on upon the air.
The bells have ceased, their last vibrations
lost along the far-spread fields. The sharp
' tzit, tzit,' of a robin, or a beetle's drone in
passing flight, seem but to intensify the
stillness. In this beautiful hour, as twilight
deepens down upon the flowers, they seem
to open their hearts to you and speak.

* 'Where are we to put the zenanas?' asked a
friend's old Scotch gardener t'other day!

The cold half-withdrawn look of common day has vanished from each lovely face, and as you pass by, voiceless, they tell you sweet nothings without words.

It is more strange than perhaps at first sight appears,—the illumination of flowers and bright coloured objects after sundown, while the green of surrounding grass and foliage is lit only with a sombre radiance. I may be pardoned for giving a suggested theory in explanation, thus : The colour of all objects depends upon the kind of illumination they receive. A completely yellow light thrown upon a nosegay will kill all colour excepting in the yellow flowers. Newton discovered that sunshine and all white lights have the power of pouring every conceivable shade of colour upon all objects, and these again have the power of extinguishing all shades except the few which suit their own substances and textures. 'A blue salvia extinguishes all the red, yellow, green, and possibly the violet rays, while a red poppy absorbs all the violet, blue, green, and possibly yellow. We therefore see

the latter brilliantly red, and the former
purely blue.' When mellowed fruits and
yellow and red flowers shine at evening
it is because the sunset light comes to
them through more and more of the
air that envelopes the earth, and which
though invisible, quenches almost entirely
the violet, blue, and green. All objects
disposed towards yellow and red are then
illuminated as with a pure light of these
two colours, and they gleam out tri-
umphantly, because all other green, blue,
and violet objects are more or less deprived
of their favourite rays. Nothing of this,
however, quite explains why white and
yellow flowers often appear so bright at
night, or why some other flowers—and
notably some kinds of crimson snap-
dragon (antirrhinum)—do often shine, so
as to attract the eye from a distance on
some very dull grey days. These (as
indeed all flowers in some degree) doubt
less have a self-luminous power, which we
call phosphorescence, whatever that may be.

We have already had large store of
delicious, well-sunned wall fruit—peaches,

figs, and plums. I can believe that, had we means to build and keep up long ranges of houses — peach houses, and nectarine and fig-houses—they would be built, and we should draw from their rich produce the same enjoyment in the same way that others do who possess glass. But I do not believe that these houses would ever give me the same delight as does the little basketful of fruit and flowers that I find placed on my table every morning on these late summer days. I do not believe that the finest fruit ripened under glass could compare at all with the beautiful red sun-ripened peaches, picked from the old brick walls! My basketful holds sometimes one such perfect peach, two or three purple figs, yellow plums bursting with sugared juice; or a golden pear, a few Muscat or Madresfield Court grapes lovely in their exquisite bloom of misty gold or black, while single flowers of richly-scented tuberose and dainty pink begonias lie intermixed with the green vine leaves and the fruits. Our sole pride of glass fruit culture is in the vinery. Season after season our grapes excel in size and in flavour. The Muscats remind me of the grapes of Italy. Travelling along the Corniche in days before railroads, grapes, large and golden-green as these are, the peasant people would bring to us and pour into our laps, with green figs and china roses all fresh and dewy. The quantity of immense bunches that are gathered out of our one small house, lasting up to nearly Christmas, never fails to be a surprise to me, although it is always the same every year.

OCTOBER

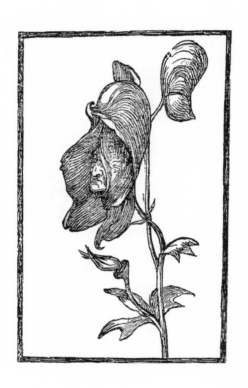

XI

OCTOBER

' Withered leaves, one—two—and three—
. . . . . .
Through the calm and frosty air
Of this morning bright and fair
Eddying round and round they sink
Softly, slowly.'

W. Wordsworth.

OCTOBER 19.—My best yellow autumn
window curtains are up! No other
curtains could ever please me so much as
these. But to make it understood how
perfect in their way they are, the windows
also must be described. They are almost
the only windows in the house that are
not old-fashioned casements. At that
period, in the beginning of the century,
when in most old houses the picturesque
and small-paned casements were made into
sash-windows, the windows of the room

I inhabit were enlarged and modernised.
Here then, are two very large sash windows,
their aspect almost due south, with the large
frames and dull bald character usual to such
windows.   Ugly as they are, they were
never altered, for the sake of the fine wide
opening made when the sash is thrown
up.   Covering the entire space of the
upper half, and enframing the whole, hang
my curtains : green for summer, and in
autumn, golden yellow.   The pair is odd,
for there must be nothing commonplace
about the room ! so the one is magnolia,
the other chiefly vine.   On the right is a
bold intricate pattern of glossy leaves with
perhaps a great white creamy blossom—
a chalice of so rich a scent—set here or
there upon the branches, with blue sky
between.   The left is all vine, made admir-
ably to suit the seasons.   In winter the
curtain is drawn back, as it were; for a
few interlacing barren lines keep out no
light.   The thin delicate arabesque of
spring gives place to summer, when the
green comes full and cool and shades
the noonday sunlight,   And now in

autumn, my left-hand curtain is all yellow
gold, reflecting back gold sunshine of its
own. There should be dispersed amid the
gold, bunches of ripe green grapes, like
clustered berylls. That part of the orna-
mental needlework ! has not been well done
this year, and the grapes are mostly shrunk
and mildewed. To repair the loss of them
slender jasmine twigs set round with
narrow dark green leaves, hold out little
silver stars, peering round the corners,
stretching round the window-sills, while
across them comes a dash of red Virginian
climber. The one fault I find, is that my
yellow curtains do not endure. Come a
sharp frost, or strong gust of wind—they
are gone in a moment.

The failure of the grapes is this year a
serious disappointment to the birds, who
count upon their vintage at the windows;
yet the shutters opening in the morning
discover them some times at work. There
is a blackbird, with full black chest,
swallowing the grapes as fast as his golden
bill can manage it; or a thrush sits in the
Vine taking breath between his mouthfuls,

while the sun shines sidelong on his spotted breast; or a robin shows his red waistcoat for a moment. He is not, I fear, my robin that has hitherto been so constant to the window—for twelve months past he has hardly missed a day. Bold and familiar in the winter, silent and hurried at nesting time—not a feather in his tail, and very shy, when moulting. Gay and *insouciant* in his new suit, looking as big again, and trilling half a bar at a time short and full, but 'always regular to his meals' at the saucer of sopped biscuit. Dear little tame robin ! I shall grieve if he is dead ; but I think he will come back in the winter, when birds are hungry. They say that robins go to the seaside in October ; and another saying would have the young birds kill the old ones at this season. Even this is better than the way my friends the swallows behave. Up to the time when they all left England— about the 13th—they seem to have been still occupied with late broods of young. It was indeed without my consent that they thus foolishly employed themselves here in the north porch. If they could but have understood, I should have persuaded them to stay a little longer, to give their young a chance. On the 16th only one swallow was seen, and three days after a tragedy happened in the porch! Late in the afternoon a poor little full-fledged swallow lay dead on the cold stones. The forsaken nestling may have fallen in its hungry efforts for food, or have attempted in its weakness to follow the stronged-winged parents, whose cruel desertion it is hard to forgive. Strange and inexplicable is the migratory instinct with birds. It is then, more powerful with them than even mother's love? and yet love is said to be stronger than death.

The habits of the swallows who make themselves at home in our entrances, north and south, are full of interest. The red-throated chimney swallows like best the north. On the south side are martins. Both kinds agree in departing from ancestral laws in their ways of house building. The typical swallow's nest used formerly to be neatly built up—usually

under the eaves—with a hole for them to
fly in and out. Our swallows of to-day
make flat hasty nests on projecting ledges
inside the porch. One nest (re-filled three
times last summer) is made up of ugly
blackish clay, bearded with long straws of
hay hanging down. Is it not a new thing
for swallows to·build with hay？ We have
only one really well-rounded neatly-finished
nest, and this is a martin's. The chimney
swallows seem to be most hurried and
careless. One of our families makes no
nest at all, there is simply a layer of mud
laid on the ledge. Along the rim the five
newly feathered young ones sit in a row to
be fed, like five little old owls in miniature.
There is one thing that a swallow never
forgets or forgives, and that is destroying
the old nests. The place remains empty
to this day where once we cleared away
two overcrowded nests. They love over-
crowding. I watched the old birds—on
their return the following May—inspect the
place, flying in and out and round about
it; but either they forsook us altogether,
or nested elsewhere about the house.

Flowers still are blooming everywhere in the garden. There are still beautiful red roses, smelling as sweet as June. Rosa rugosa has only just ceased to flower. A great clump of pale blush anemone japonica at the south end of the broad walk has flowered grandly for some time past. A clump of white ones from the kitchen garden is to be planted there also, since it is plain that they look best in large masses. Had we room I should like to plant blue salvia next to the white anemones. The fine blue of this old salvia enriches now the whole garden in almost every part. The colour is said by some to be in a false key, and as such to be out of tune with the more natural greens and blues around, contrasting ill with the lovely tones of nemophila or of the blue daisy— or even with the firmament itself! I know not how this may be, but to me it is nevertheless a magnificent blue—nearest, perhaps, in tone to the deep blue of the alpine gentian, and losing beside the gentian only because it lacks its depth of jetty heart. Pure ultramarine must be

used in the painting of either flower. Our
old walls are all well-furnished with the
vivid orange-scarlet glow of tropæolum.
It gives promise, too, of lasting on as long
as winter frosts delay. I cannot give the
name of this special variety of Tropæolum,
or nasturtium is it? Its leaf is bluish
and round, and the plant seems to be
always in flower, from August until far
into November.

In the entrance court the old useless green gages and golden drop plum
trees against the walls are dressed out in
these gay flowers, climbing, streaming,
creeping, clustering about all over them,
branch and stem. The vivid colouring
is splendid; it seems but a few days
since it mixed in many places with the
purple of Jackman's clematis. At this
moment the blossoms intermingle here
and there with tall, yellow helianthus.
The aged fruit trees are doomed, and
flowering climbers are to cover the walls
in their place. The standard cherry tree
between the pyramid yews is to be cut
down, and a broader flower border to be

made. It is hard to sentence the cherry
tree! In spring it is so like a great
round nosegay of loveliest blossom, and
when the cherries begin to redden a
thrush so loves to build its nest in it,
and at evening to perch on the top and
sing the lingering day away. Yet the
cherry tree must go. These kind of
changes which at intervals have to be
made throughout the garden cause us
a thousand regrets. When the young
trees and shrubs thrive and grow all
round as Nature intended, the very success and growth of them overturns all
our plans, and changes are inevitable.
'The Fantaisie' has changed its character
and is not the same in any way as it was
when first laid out. Then, flowers and
evergreen shrubs grew together on either
side the turf walk, and each enhanced
the other's charm. Twelve or thirteen
years later the cryptomerias and aucubas
and berberis have grown so large, that
nearly all the flowers are crowded out,
and a new aspect takes possession of the
whole. The law of change which thus

rules the garden has lately forced us to remove a large English yew from the spot which it has occupied for many years. It was pushing its dark growth right into the beautiful grey foliage of an Abies amabilis. So last month the grand move had to be arranged.

To watch the transplanting of a tree is a choice amusement of autumn in the garden. The work begins early in the morning. Two, three, four hours or more, according to the size of the tree, is taken up with digging round and throwing out the earth. The roots and rootlets have to be carefully separated : not cut or severed more than is necessary. The tree is tied close with strong cords : all its lower branches bound up together. The head gardener watches and gives his orders quietly, jumps down into the trench, and lends a hand himself with spade or pick : walking round, returning again and again. Silently, cheerfully, the men work. A wholesome fragrance of new earth spreads upwards in the air. The labour is severe, but at last the tree stands free, with a great

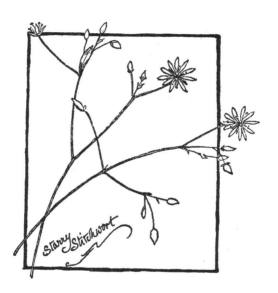

Starry Stitchwort

ball of earth round his roots. The bell goes for the men's dinner; powdered all over with brown mould they scramble up and shake themselves, throw an old mat over the roots, and depart for their hour of rest. The men return refreshed, and set to work again with a will; and now three tall stout poles, the ends meeting at top in a triangle, are set up and fixed, with ropes and pulleys fastened to them. It may take long to adjust all right, but at last the tree swings high in the air, dangling from the summit of the triangle. The excitement of the moment grows intense. Two or three men in the pit below steady and guide the ascending mass; four or five pull the ropes with might and main. The tree swings fair above the centre of a trolley, wheeled up to the edge ready to receive it. The Gardener holds on to the strong shaft or handle of the trolley, his eye fixed anxiously on the swaying tree, encouraging the men, directing every movement. The ropes are tight; the tree is well up. 'Now let go! slacken the ropes!—gently—so!' Gently the tree is lowered down upon the platform of the trolley, and the ball of earth once more is wrapt in mats.

Now begins the dragging, and pushing, and pulling; there's a shove and a tug all together, and the tree is fairly off on its journey. Toiling along the gravel-walks, the triumphal car rolls slowly on. The progress may be short or long; somewhere it ends, at the edge of a big hole prepared in the special spot designated to receive the tree. Soon he slides safely down into the bed ready made in the hole. There is a merry shovelling in and stamping of the earth, leaving a little ditch all round to hold the great watering which is the ending of the work; and there the tree is left, looking as if he had been there all his life. Unmoved the neighbouring trees and shrubs stand round, and not a green leaf flutters welcome to the new-comer; it is henceforth as if the transplanted tree had never been anywhere else. Should the tree we have to move be larger than usual, it may take to do it twenty-six working hours or more.

Men of old time planted trees for pos-
terity.   With far-seeing wisdom they
planned many a stately avenue, which
still remain the ornament and pride of our
fine old country houses.   We do not in
these days seem always to look so far
beyond the present.   When a few years
ago I planted a row of young limes (in
old books they are 'lines') as a continua-
tion of the lime avenue, with arbor-vitæ
between each tree, and parellel to these a
double row of larch, and a beech hedge
along the walk between the limes and the
larch—I did not foresee the dilemma that
has ensued.   A decision must before long
be made between the selfish enjoyment of
the present, extending perhaps to a few
uncertain years, or the future and lasting
improvement of the place, which I shall
not see.   While we hesitate the trees grow
on.   The stems of the limes grow thick
and smooth, and their branches spread ;
the beautiful green arbor-vitæ flourish,
and are rapidly making handsome trees ;
my favourite larch send up strong tall
shoots every season threatening to over-

whelm everything; while the beech hedge is so luxuriant that I am tempted to sacrifice all to it. Which is it to be?

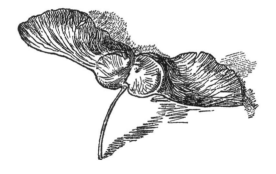

M

' WHY should we sorrow,
   That summer's dazzling ray
   So soon has passed away ?
   Whilst we can borrow,
   From Autumn's yellow light
   A scene more purely bright ?

' Where'er the eye can wander,
   The garden and the field,
   A richer prospect yield.
   Earth seems to squander
   Her plenty in the sheaf
   Her gold in ev'ry leaf.'

NOVEMBER

XII

NOVEMBER

'Change and decay in all around I see,
O Thou who changest not abide with me.'

J. Newman.

'The spirit culls
Unfaded amaranth, when wild it strays
Through the old garden ground of boyish days.'

J. Keats.

NOVEMBER 30, 1887.—November is going
out with all the soft warmth of a summer
month. On such a day as this, the gum
cistus gives out its sweetness, and the
aroma of its leaves floats past upon the
milk-warm wind. I found to-day upon
a grass walk a wind-snapt branch of it,
and holding it in my hand as I walked,
the garden seemed all wrapt in delicious
airs as from some sweet southern clime.
There are roses too: real pink roses in

the garden, full blown, and full of summer
fragrance.   And tea-roses are showing
large firm swelling buds which look as if
come what might, they were resolved to
open.   Little white blossoms shine amongst
the wood strawberry leaves under the
south windows.   Ferns still are freshly
green : only here and there they are
changing colour in groups of orange,
russet-brown and gold.   Growing among
the ' rocks ' on the Roman Walk, a plant of
yellow Sysirhinchium which has flowered
persistently during the past six months,
still points with primrose yellow its narrow
reed-like leaves.   The glory of the garden
is the Christmas rose.   Our one great
healthy clump is, in the heart of it,
silvered all over with the promise of finer
bloom than it has ever been known to
show.   It means to bloom rather earlier
than usual this season, and as yet has no
bower of fir branches built over it to
ward off the frost.   Scarcely the least
tinge of red in any one of the score of
well opened blossoms mars as yet their
perfect white.

Beautiful as they are, we do not often gather them for the house, for when parted from their own dark foliage, Christmas roses lose always a part of their life and spirit ; and yet the leaves look too coarse when cut, and besides being difficult to arrange, to cut them off from the plant will often seriously wound it. I have tried to arrange with them sprays of flexiosa honeysuckle embrowned with winter, but nothing really answers. Chrysanthemums on the other hand, seem made for 'decking up the house' just now ! They are brilliant in white and yellow and chocolate brown and all the indescribable tints we know and love so well. But our dear Christmas roses are best left among the dead leaves, growing in the earth where they love to be, and there they gladden our eyes with un-looked - for joy, when summer's flight makes the heart sad. The purple coloured and green Hellebores that were sent us from the north, hardly do their best here. They are budding well, but they are rather unwilling denizens, and wear the look of existing here only as specimens. Notwithstanding the unusual warmth, the garden in these late November days is dull and sorrowful. Broken, blackened wrecks of past delight, strewed over every part of it, seem to impart a more than common gloom. The sense of ' change and decay,' pervades the very air about us, as we traverse the garden paths, along by the ruined shrubberies and borders, or pass near haunted, grassy ways.

There is always a certain charm in the curious mosaic of autumn leaves, lying as they fall, this way and that, across each other on every side. Leaves are mostly sure to fall picturesquely, and to die off in fine shades of brown and tawny red. And yet, unless in frosty weather, when they rustle deliciously under foot, there is a feeling of damp discomfort about them ! the leaves of Occidental plane and of American oak shew the most variety of colour : while, the large foliage of polygonum, when withered and scattered about like huge fragments of brown paper, is, I think, downright ugly !

How surely does autumn give a tinge of melancholy to a garden reverie! and how the feeling grows with age! But it is not like the ideal sorrowfulness of youth, that dwells so marvellous sweet in our remembrance. It is simply that we listen now to the shortened step of the years to come; it is only that now, we feel and we know, how for us the days are numbered that will bring back the flowers in their season. Even the lilac bunches of autumn crocus, both double and single, which arise here and there on the bare earth without any green about them do not make much cheer. My pleasant paths are all forlorn; the singing birds are flown or dead, and unbroken silence reigns in the unleaved thickets they once loved so well. There are no delightful surprises now; quite plainly and bare of all disguise we see the empty nest in the fork of many a leafless branch; nests, to discover which in the green June days, we used to peep about and part the leaves or peer into the heart of the yew hedge, so very unsuccessfully!

Never do I remember the pinched and hanging stalks and blackened mouldered ruins of summer, to have made the garden look more drearily disconsolate. Yet even now, in the mournfullest wreck-encumbered borders, straight slender stems appear already full of greenest sap and of 'all the wonder that's to be.' As the saying goes, 'when one door shuts another opens.' And so though a thousand regretful memories cling round the autumn garden, and rise in the heart with the scent of dead and dying leaves, there is no time to dwell on them. Winter's happy working day begins. Now is the time to play all manner of new invented games with flower beds and borders, lawns and shrubberies. The laying out of lines in a garden is not perhaps so easy as might be thought. Your design may look well on paper but when actually cut out in the turf, most likely it will come all wrong; and the clearest head will find too late, that essential details of surroundings have been forgot, or not sufficiently taken into account. The work of remodelling our entrance

court has in this way been a lesson. It
was so hard to get the curves and angles
right, and to make the lines fit in,—chiefly
it must be admitted by reason of irregularity
in the old walls. A cherry tree, a straggling
old apple, and some worn out greengages
against the wall all taken away, have made
the trimmed pyramid yews look larger;
each yew now stands out in solid blackness
from his setting of rounded turf. And now
lovely clamberers must be chosen for the
old brick walls denuded of their fruit trees.
There must certainly be blue ceanothus
and a passion flower, and above all a
scarlet pyracanthus.

I know not what curious thread of far-
off association gives this common wall-tree
its fascination, at least for myself. I only
know the peculiar thrill that invariably
startles me whenever I see one covered
with ripe fruit. There is a pyracanthus
trained up the common wooden paling of
a little roadside dwelling that I often have
to pass. Familiarity affects not the kind
of shock of satisfaction which the sight of
its orange red berries never fails to bring.

It is something like, when in music a minor chord drops at once into the full major harmony. So without doubt a pyracanthus must be planted. Only now, in the gloom and damp, we seem to know the full value of scarlet geranium. There are a goodly number of them grown under glass in the frames, and never in the hottest days in August have such scarlet splendours shot from the blossoms. They absolutely flash red rays of burning fire from the glasses on the table. Fireball we find the best for cutting in November. Henri Jacobi is too sombre. Vesuvius is gaiety itself, but Fireball is best. A few starry gold-eyed marguerites, should be mixed in, and there must be no leaves ; the stalks of tender green showing all criss-cross within the clear glass, are relief enough. A glass full of such brilliant colour as this, will illumine the dulness of the gloomiest mid-winter day.

———

Thus far goes my garden diary of 1887. This 30th of November four years after, is cold and damp and shrouded in a thick white fog. There have been troublous times of wet and wind with alternating frosts. The earth is saturated with moisture : so much so that the very worms are made uncomfortable in it, and wriggle up to the outer air, making tracks across the wet walks where they lie at last all pale and watery, and somewhat unpleasanter than usual.

Change and decay in the garden have gone on the same. The passion flower and the blue ceanothus were planted, bloomed and flourished for a season, and then last winter perished in the frost. The red pyraneanthus planted with them is in its place, all scarlet, and netted from the birds. About the middle of the month a great south wind raged for all one night and day, and our one young American oak fell, snapped close to the root : so there is an end of the rich autumnal foliage which had been a joy each year while it lived with us. A yet greater loss is one of the mighty elms, in the house meadow. It broke right in half, and fell with such violence that big limbs of it dug into the tennis lawn and there stuck fast several feet deep. The tree measured (half of it standing firm and half stretched on the turf), over 120 feet, and all of it fine sound-hearted timber. It must have been soon after that, I went out to enjoy the tremendous music of the storm, raging in the tops of the elms, and watched the old accacia rock and heave up and down from the very roots. It seemed as though every heave might be its last. For on every side but one the roots had entirely given way. It did not altogether go that day. But the poor old accacia tree is sentenced, and before winter ends the axe will have laid it low. Yet one cannot but feel sorry for the nuthatches! no other tree will afford them with such conveniently rough bark, for the cracking of their nuts. Up to last week the garden has been full of roses. Pink and crimson and creamy tea-roses, all sweet as summer, and quite unheeding of the weather. Even York and Lancasters have tried their best to bloom, and made some sickly little flowers, which were picked off the moment they appeared. We have had bowls full of my favourite china roses, both pink and crimson.

NOVEMBER 30TH 1893.—Last summer our roses did well, although some other gardens told a different story. A new long border was cleared and planted with a great many of the best new roses : very choice and wholly uninteresting. For that new border I had been very anxious to procure what some one just returned from New York, described as 'Jack roses.' I was told they were of a fine crimson red and very profuse bloomers. But these turned out to be nothing but the well-known old General Jackminot, which with the usual love for abbreviation in the United States has come to be simply 'Jack.' The disappointment was soon forgotten in the many rose treasures we have since possessed. Socrates, a lovely rose that hated the border is removed to the greenhouse, where is a healthy Camellia Rose, making vigorous shoots both long and strong. It takes a very large flower pot now; early in March the lovely white single blossoms will begin to open all over it, their fragrance exquisite and unlike to any other rose,—and the perfume seems to live within the centre of its yellow stamens. Then we move out the great pot with its load of loveliness, and it is placed in the shade well sheltered from the wind, to be a joy and delight for full three weeks. This spring, she stood out side by side with a fine pot-plant of Fortune's yellow. The sister roses were both so beautiful one scarce knew which to admire most. I do not think the Camellia Rose (Japan) is often seen in English gardens, but on the Riviera it has long been familiar. At Cannes, the Villa Grand Bois is half covered with it. And in the gardens of La Mortola between Menton and Ventimiglia, memory recalls with delight long lovely garlands of it enwreathing the low thickets of rose and aloe. In the frames we have nearly half a score of charming little shrubby roses grown from Indian seed. The flowers as yet are very small, but highly scented and deep in colour, keeping

their rich pink when dried. Lucille, an old-
fashioned climber—famous for the charm
of its bud—promises well on the wire rose-
arches. To these have been lately added
the long-desired old Celestial rose and the
Jacobite white rose. This last is a gift
straight from a garden in the Chanonry,
Aberdeen Old Town, where 'it has always
been,' as one says. It is the very rose
they loved and wore for Prince Charlie.
Rosa cinnamomea (the Willow rose),
grows most luxuriantly with us, and even
threatens to become tiresome. Its flowers
are marked by the lovely peculiarity of a
little round pink pointal. Yet even as I
write, a doubt arises whether after all it *is*
really cinnamomea! or whether it be not
rather rosa pomefera major, the great
Apple Rose of Parkinson. Portions of his
description of each would suit in part either
of these two roses, while a third 'the
rose without thorns,' or the 'marbled
rose,' is still more like.

I would not quarrel with my Parkinson;
but certainly his descriptions of the roses
of his day, are perhaps somewhat involved.

N

Our Willow rose might in these days be thus described :—' Smooth long stems with infrequent thorns at intervals set singly or in pairs, tufted with narrow willow-shaped leaves in the midst of which appear the flowers, five-petalled, of a full pink colour. In the centre of each flower a little round pink button or pointal surrounded by yellow stamens. The hips are dark red and round like little russet pippins, and these tiny apples being hairy while young, become in time quite smooth and shining.' There exist no doubts, however, about the Velvet rose (Rosa tholoserica simplex et multiplex). A few plants of this neglected rose, survive in our older shrubberies, the flower is neatly made and small : semi-double, of a deep, black-crimson colour, and velvety with yellow threads. The velvet rose is not very good for cutting, as it never lasts. Yet by its so great abundance in the season of its bloom, I am always tempted to gather of it. The Ayrshire rose has been added to our store, but as yet the rooted cuttings have not left their nursery.

In all the garden there are but two bushes of pink Cabbage rose. The North seems to greatly favour this old beauty. All through August last and a part of September, roadside cottage gardens on Deeside were ideal, with a perfumed pink profusion of them. Everywhere rows of large untidy bushes were seen hung all over with round and heavy roses. Just one remnant of a Crested rose (once so fashionable), survives, I believe, somewhere among the Rhododendrons in the Boccage. I discovered it by chance two years ago ; but somehow it slipt away again before that summer ended, and it has never since been seen. The little Rose de Meaux too—joy of our childhood—has disappeared from the border where once it grew, and so has the Fairy Rose disappeared from the kitchen garden. I have heard of little hedges of the Fairy rose instead of box edgings. But amongst all the roses of other days, the Celestial rose is surely queen ! The little round Burnet Roses, white and yellow, are sweetest of all.

In the east border, under the wall, two

grand old Baron Prevost, are covered with
a second bloom, or rather their bloom has
never ceased all summer long. These trees
are over six feet in height, having been
originally worked on a stem as tree roses. I
have known them for upwards of twenty-
six years. But the name of the Celestial
sets me dreaming of the loveliness of many
a half-forgotten rose of our grandmothers'
gardens : and musing, appears before me
like a dream, an old Scotch garden as I
saw it on a July day a year ago—and hope
again to see it summer by summer.

It is just an old-fashioned Scotch kitchen
garden within a beechwood—full of fine
potatoes and turnips and berries, and
flower borders. Two acres gently sloping
to the south, enclosed within lofty grey
granite walls which are almost hidden
behind ancient cherry, pear, and apple
trees. The granite walls enclose three
sides, and the fourth, the south side, is
picturesquely fenced, though the fencing
may be unpropitious enough for a kitchen
garden. A low stone wall with narrow
tall brick pillars rising above it at intervals

and a woodwork trellis of faded green
between each. The trellis is heavily overgrown with great masses of ivy and
honeysuckle — white honeysuckle just
now in richest bloom and fragrance—and
is partly hidden by the wild growth of a
neglected shrubbery border where tall
white campanula and Aaron's rod,
Solomon's seal, and weedy Turk's cap
lilies, struggle to the light through a
wilderness of guelder rose and spindle,
and holly and gean trees.

Pushing open the door, between the
heavy granite door posts quite over-
canopied with honeysuckle, and with the
gooseberry and raspberry and snow-
berry, that for many a year have seeded
and grown up in unheeded luxuriance
from every cranny in the stones—the plan
of the garden is disclosed at once. It
is very simple : a long straight walk
between borders of turf and flowers and
two hedges of cotoneaster, leading up to
a green door at the other end ; a walk
all round, and four cross walks. After
the true old Scotch style, each walk is

bordered with flowers and gooseberry and currant bushes, roses and columbines, with a thousand other less familiar plants beside. But the old - fashioned roses are the glory and the charm of the garden. Long before La France was born, or Gloire de Dijon's name was heard, these beautiful gay damasks and York and Lancasters, grew and flourished here. And strange to say, here their old titles also have survived.

Two tall sweet briers guard the entrance of the brier cross-walk. To-day they are *covered* with little pink roses, like nothing I have ever seen since Masaccio's fresco in the Ricardi palace at Florence, where rose-crowned angels kneel in a row beside a low rose hedge. One knows not on which side to look, so splendid on either hand is the array of roses, red and white ; heavy - headed cabbage roses, roses of Provence and pink moss roses in the wildest profusion. The crimson damask are so ' brode ' as old garden-writers say, so vigorous, so replete with colour and with fragrance, they literally glow like

crimson lamps of fire, whenever the sky
is overcast. Broad roses, indeed they are,
for the least of them will measure five
inches across with ten great petals and
smaller ones besides, around the centre
diadem of bright gold stamens, from the
midst of which rises the stiff, thick column
of clustered pistil. It is difficult to see or
smell or to write of these damasks without an enthusiasm that seems to carry
one away! Fine clumps of English iris
vary with their exquisite tints of lilac
or violet and speckled mauve, the all-
prevailing rose-red pink and white. This
iris is far more Scotch than English, for
there is scarce a cottage garden round
about in Aberdeenshire without its iris
clumps. I know a little garden there,
that grows them in a wonderful double
line, milk-white. 'Aye,' responds the
gudewife when the great number of her
white flowers is admired, ' I just slice 'em
like ing'ons (onions) and digs them in.'
And beside the irises, thrives in deep
fiery crimson, a certain double dwarf Sweet
William—the gardener's pride—and the

clear amber-yellow of low-growing œnothera. Here too, is Sauguinaria Canadensis.

A faint scent of bergamot leads you to
a plant or two of purplish Fraxinella.
Pass your hand across the leaves, and the
perfume will cling to it ; or come again
after dark and strike a match under its
nose ! and the flowers will blaze up and
crackle and be none the worse. Purple
Canterbury bells as big as coffee cups with
saucers too, contrast beautifully with the
almost ethereal purity of the great white
Cabbage, or Provence, roses, which toss
themselves in singular confusion of crossing
bud and bloom. I believe this last
came out anew last year as the York rose.
Years ago, it was the Neapolitan rose.
Could she but open her petals more tidily
she would be supreme. Great bushes of it
alternate in another walk with old pink
cabbage and moss roses. The former has
such a heavy head that one needs must
hold it up to look within at the round,
pink, bird's nest. And then it strikes one
at once, that this was the type of the rose
of ancient sculpture—of the Cathedral at

Amiens : and also of Mary Moser's crayons, and of the once fashionable papier-mâché tea-trays, and card-board painted hand-screens, and all the rest of the flower-art of that period when the century was young. But now the brier walk leads into the broad side walk, and here begins the reign of Velvet roses, sweetest of them all, though they last for but one brief day or so. The flower is made of real silk velvet leaves, full of delicious fragrance, wine-dark in colour. The learned dispute about which was the Velvet rose. But the guardian of this old Scotch garden has no such doubts; 'This' he says 'is the Velvet rose.' Just for the pleasure of hearing them, I like to pretend ignorance, and ask him for the name of this or that rose. Quite naturally, and without hesitation he will answer, 'the Velvet rose,' or 'the damask,' or 'the white cabbage,' etc., as if they were the modernest roses !

Here and there the finer pink of a care-less, semi-double flower, marks an un-named variety, nearly allied to the crested rose. On the shady side of the garden, among the potatoes, distinguished by its grace of growth, by its bluish-green leaf, and its half single snow-white flower, we know the ancient Jacobite rose. Until I knew its name, it used to seem so strange, that in some parts, never a roadside cottage, or little muirland dwelling, if no more than a 'butt and a ben,' but has its white rose bush growing by the door, or straggling across the dyke. It is the old Jacobite rose, and its presence thus surviving still among us, is a living link with those far off troubled times, when Prince Charlie was the darling of the people, and his rose, the 'rose that's like the sna',' was planted by every house-wall in that north land of loyalty. They had their white rose always near, though they might not dare to wear it. One other forgotten rose of beauty, the oft named Celestial, is recalled by the shapely oval bud of the Jacobite. Every old rose has its special attribute or character. The attribute of this, is an exquisite neatness, combined with the most consummate loveliness. Though impossible to paint it in words, it is like this : — Leaves cold blue-green, evenly serrated. The bud, packed as if by hand (a fairy's hand!) opens slowly, leaf by leaf. The open flower is almost flat, and forms into a perfect circle, suffused with a delicious pink, which is like no other pink. They did well who named it rose of Heaven, for other roses come not near to equal the fairness of it—faultless in its purity of shape and colour.

How few remember now that lovely flower : like many another sweet old thing —it has gone out of fashion. New roses give so little real pleasure! They are so often without scent ; and is not the fragrance of it, the rose's soul? But I know little of them, and incline to rank them with exhibition chrysanthemums, which one loathes. Sometimes, however, it is, I confess, love at first sight. It was so when first I saw 'Lady Folkestone'— and the so-called 'white La France.' These two came to live in the garden, and I hope never to lose the charm of their fair beauty. Once in a vision I saw a rose ! I believe it has never bloomed or earth ; but perhaps it may come some happy day among the newly invented briers. It was a single-flowered white rose the petals delicately edged with pink.

DECEMBER

XIII

DECEMBER

' The steadfast mind that to the end
  Is fortune's victor still,
Hath yet a fear, though Fate befriend,
  A hope though all seem ill.
Jove can at will the winter send,
  Or call the spring at will.'
William Watson (Odes of Horace).

DECEMBER 24TH.—There are roses, real
pink roses, full blown in the garden still.
Tea roses also are there, showing large
firm buds which look resolved to open.
There are little white strawberry blossoms
shining among the wild strawberry leaves
in the south border under the windows of
the house. 'All is seeming, nothing is,'
at the season of this nigh two thousand
year old anniversary. And thus in the
days long gone by, a dream like this I
dreamed :—

XIV

ON CHRISTMAS EVE

A Mother's Dream

CHRISTMAS was with us, almost before we were aware, and the Christmas tree had not yet been cut in the Fir wood. Soon it would be carried home to be decked in burning lights and tinsel toys. And the children began to ask, ' Mother, where are we to have the Christmas tree?' and she made answer quietly, 'In the wood, to-night.' But the elder children were displeased; and one said the night was cold, and another said the way was slippery, and none of them would leave the warm fireside. And so the children agreed they would not go out to find the Christmas tree in the dark wood. Only the little one, the boy with the fair round face and the flowing hair—he softly stole his hand into his mother's, and looking up in her eyes, he said, 'I will go with you!' So they went out both of them together into the still starlight. The night was clear and cold and the little one must have his fur hood, and the warm cloak must be closely wrapped round him. And they went down the steps into the garden and so across the lawn through the narrow gate into the wild dark wood. And the child's eyes were full of wonder as he saw the great golden stars above the trees, and knew not they were God's eternal word written in the heavens.

Silently we went on our way. The green moss under our feet, the bare black stems of ancient forest trees rising up on either hand, till we came where two paths crossed, and there, at the entering in of the wood where the fir trees began—stood three Angels. They were clad in moon-white raiment, and crowned with roses, pure roses of Paradise, whose far off fragrance stirred our very heart.

The countenance of the angels was but dimly seen, by reason of a dazzling glory round their heads—yet, it seemed as though they smiled, and beckoned to us with the hand. A gentle wind arose and swayed

o

the branches over head—and there was
the sound of murmurous music amid
the pines. And deeper and further into
the deep wood the child and I passed
onward, silently hand in hand, and many
fair trees we passed by, but found not the
tree we sought. And about the middle of
the way, the three angels parted from us,
and afar off shone a beautiful light, and it
seemed to me that we saw very nigh the
light of the Christmas tree ! But as we
drew more near, behold it was not the tree
but a bright star shining low in the wood.
And now I knew not any longer where we
were, for the trees were about us no
more, but only a wide moonlit mountain
land.

Cold moonbeams whitened the flocks
upon a thousand hills, and the Star had
paled its light in the glory streaming forth
from the open door of a lowly ruined hut
beneath it. The radiance grew and grew
until there was not any more night. And
then, with our eyes we beheld the Virgin
Mother ; and her Holy Child lay beside
her in the manger ; and the ox and the

ass were there. The shepherds also were kneeling at His feet.

Then we two in the outer blackness drew very near and trembled. And filled with joy, and with rapturous awe, we knelt with the shepherds of Bethlehem, and we gazed at the babe through tears of love and holy fear. And while we gazed, a note of utter sweetness rose and swelled until it became like the solemn sound of an organ, until it filled all the place where we were, and shook the walls of the lowly cattle shed bursting and shattering up through the roof. And there was a rushing sound as of innumerable multitudes of angels' wings, and they were like sharp-pointed flames of fire thronging all around and upward. In our ears we heard pealing and echoing, and dying away amidst the hills, the words of the ancient song of Peace, 'Glory to God, and Peace on earth.' We hid our faces in our hands, and so the vision departed from our sight, and the fir trees closed in once more around us. So dreamfully we wandered on, the child's face all glowing yet, and bright with the shining of the heavenly light that we had seen, his cheek still wet with happy tears.

Low in the valley where in spring we found the subtle-scented primroses, and where snow-drops make soft moonlight under the trees in early days of March, there, in an open space at last we saw the Christmas Tree.

Alone under the starry sky the Tree burnt with a great glow of golden fruits amid the living fire of myriads of precious stones, all glorious from the lowest to the topmost branch, making in that shady place so great a splendour that we could see the little birds with their heads turned under their wing-feathers, sleeping in the winter trees. The light awoke them not, but round the trees soft wild furry creatures, with merry, jet-black eyes, peeped here and there. And here and there crept from underneath some stone or withered leaf, the slow toad, with a glittering jewel in her head. In and out amongst the shining lights played little flashes of emerald green.

Strange wonder with a delicious surprise held the child's lips that he could not speak. And the mother gently led him by the hand up to the beauteous tree, and pointing to the ripe living fruits that hung thereon, she whispered : 'They are yours !' They were of such kinds as ripen not in earthly gardens. The radiance and the colours of them shone from a heavenly land, where grow unchecked the fruits of love and joy and peace, of wisdom and of eternal life and innocence. Wreathed about the branches were garlands of the freshest flowers, pure flowers of meekness and gentleness and long-suffering and truth. And amidst of these immortal flowers and fruit, half hidden by their bloom, far far up beyond our reach, hung many crowns of divers kinds—jewelled crowns of delight, and rainbow crowns of fancy, white cold snow-crowns, and royal crowns of fire, and pale crowns of fear—and silvery chains festooned with pearls which are tears . . . But on all these we set not our eyes. For near the very summit of the green pyramid of glory, hung one beautiful flower-crown—

rose-hued and fire-hearted even in that clear midnight, the Crown of Love out-shone the very stars in heaven. And I cried, 'Oh my little one, let us reach down to us the Crown of Love.' And then they stretched out their arms, though the love-crown hung so far above. . . . And suddenly the sky was overcast and heavy clouds hid all the stars. And a shuddering blast swept past through the wood spreading wide the child's long hair . . . . and the fair fruits and the garlands fell from the Christmas Tree, and the rose leaves were blown away and scattered, and the place was filled with a wild storm of sweetness.

One only diadem remained, while all the rest had faded, even as an evening mist shimmering through the ruined roses; and the wind shook the trees, so that the Love-crown floated down to us. But even then as with eager hand we seemed to grasp them, the flowers were not ; but the thorns of the Crown of Pain pierced through the mother's heart as she clasped it close, and the rose leaves became drops.

of blood. Then I turned in anguish to my child. But he had folded his hands unhurt upon his breast, and gazed smiling, with joyful eyes upon those sharp naked thorns. And she knew that the little one perceived only the Divine and pearly radiance, which for her, shone as a dim halo of tears around the crimsoned wreath . . . . Gathered in her arms the mother held the child for a moment, there, in the dewy twilight of a green Christmas dawn : while far-heard Christmas bells awoke the day to love and holy joy. And the night had departed like a by-gone dream. And there, with tender-taken breath slept my little one beside me, and a pure white rose-bud lay upon the pillow. At the window a robin sang a short, sweet carol to the breaking day.

XV

CHRISTMAS DAY

EX UMBRA *

' IN twilight while I walk alone
    A strange voice calls me, clear and low ;
A shadowy hand that seeks my own,
    Cold as the wind and soft as snow,
Still leads me, leads me as I pass
    Across the grey December grass.

' The village windows beckon still
    With glow of amber and of gold ;
But my way lies along the hill,
    My road must cross the frosty wold ;
And still I feel and still I see
    The darkness round me deep and free.'

IN the dark, clear, early morning, the
thrushes are singing with soft under
voices.   At this early hour before sunrise
they are not afraid, and many a dear
speckled breast and swelling throat is
plainly to be seen in the elms and limes,
on branches overhanging the road.

* By permission of Editor *Pall Mall Gazette.*

A white Christmas is beautiful, but I think I like almost better the soft warm grey which the wild birds love. There is a feeling that underneath the dim grass comes then a stirring of life: that the snowdrops and crocuses are feeling upwards and are ready to break through to the light.

Poor birds! Poor little flowers! It is all a dream, and the worst of winter is to come: soon or late it has to be, and January will have no pity.

What would life be without Hope? How should we endure the melancholy of the Iris ground at this moment, covered as it is with apparently decaying roots and broken rubbish of wet, dead leaves, did not the mind's eye see it in its glow of summer bloom, as we hope to see it a few months hence! Beside the narrow aqueduct that runs down to us from the village ponds a mile distant (and which is always dry except in winter when it is not wanted) a plantation of Japanese iris Kœmpferi has been made :—that is, they were meant to be the Japanese, but when they arrived from Holland they turned out to be mostly another sort, with narrow leaves and smaller flowers. Nevertheless they are very charming with their varieties of pure white and lilac and purple, and some of the white have broad petals, although their leaves are narrow. The place is too dry for them to succeed perfectly : the Kœmpferi should grow close to the water, by a lake or a stream. I have laboured hard for them, however, collecting stones and wheeling them (in an old perambulator) and planting them about the roots to keep whatever moisture there may be.

In stones, I have the greatest faith. I like to arrange them with my own hands, round the roots I love the most. It may be fancy, but yet a pleasant fancy dashed with truth, that many a lovely favourite has been thus saved from withering death. The moss-roses love these stones ! So does a curious red-brown iris which made no flowers for three years after being transplanted from its own old home in the West. Yet there are several plants who refuse to be comforted, or to believe that the stones I give to them are bread! Iris Susiana— grand, melancholy, bizarre, half-mourning iris!—once flowered magnificently in the garden. But that was five or six years ago. Since then, excepting in the greenhouse, she has shown no sign of any wish to bloom. No careful choice of situation, no sheltering with glass during October and November has yet availed to move her rigid self-reserve. Ground up lime-stone mixed well with the soil might be a help. The strong mixture of granite in the soil of Scotch gardens may be perhaps the secret of the vigour and strength of colour and larger size of their flowers, compared with ours. In Riviera gardens, the black iris luxuriates. Long ago in one of these gardens by the sea, groups of it in full flower grew on the green margin of a little pool of water. Half hidden among the great leaves stood a low stone sun-dial, whose motto round about it went thus: 'Vado e vengo, ogni giorno, ma tu andrai senza ritorno.' The music of the words still seems to haunt the soul in opal tinted dreams, whose colour somehow does not fade with the fading light of other days.

Snowflake
from the Thames

.

For EU product safety concerns, contact us at Calle de José Abascal, 56–1°,
28003 Madrid, Spain or eugpsr@cambridge.org.

www.ingramcontent.com/pod-product-compliance
Ingram Content Group UK Ltd.
Pitfield, Milton Keynes, MK11 3LW, UK
UKHW010338140625
459647UK00010B/672